RENEWING PHILOSOPHY

RENEWING PHILOSOPHY

Hilary Putnam

HARVARD UNIVERSITY PRESS

Cambridge, Massachusetts
London, England

Library of Congress Cataloging-in-Publication Data
Putnam, Hilary.
    Renewing philosophy / Hilary Putnam.
        p.   cm.
    Includes bibliographical references and index.
    ISBN 0-674-76093-X (alk. paper) (cloth)
    ISBN 0-674-76094-8 (pbk.)
    1. Philosophy.   2. Philosophy and science.   I. Title.
B29.P88   1992
100—dc20   92-10854
                                                CIP

For Erika, Samuel, Joshua, and Polly (Max)

Contents

Preface

The present book grew out of the Gifford Lectures, which I delivered at the University of St. Andrews in the Fall of 1990, and, with one exception, its chapters are quite close to the lectures as given. (Chapter 5 has been very substantially rewritten. In addition, there was an opening lecture in which, perhaps perversely, I chose to deal with the present situation in quantum mechanics and its philosophical significance, which I decided did not really belong with the others.)

At first blush, the topics with which the lectures dealt may seem to have little relation to one another: I spoke of reference and realism and religion and even of the foundations of democratic politics. Yet my choice of these topics was not an arbitrary one. I was guided, of course, by my own past areas of concern, since it would have been foolish to lecture on topics on which I had not done serious thinking and writing in the past, but beyond that I was guided by a conviction that the present situation in philosophy is one that calls for a revitalization, a renewal, of the subject. Thus this book, in addition to addressing several topics individually, offers a diagnosis of the present situation in philosophy as a whole and suggests the directions in which we might look for such a renewal. That suggestion does not take the form of a manifesto, however, but rather takes the form of a series of reflections on various philosophical ideas.

Analytic philosophy has become increasingly dominated by

the idea that science, and only science, describes the world as it is in itself, independent of perspective. To be sure, there are within analytic philosophy important figures who combat this scientism: one has only to mention Peter Strawson, or Saul Kripke, or John McDowell, or Michael Dummett. Nevertheless, the idea that science leaves no room for an independent philosophical enterprise has reached the point at which leading practitioners sometimes suggest that all that is left for philosophy is to try to anticipate what the presumed scientific solutions to all metaphysical problems will eventually look like. (This is accompanied by the weird belief that one *can* anticipate that on the basis of *present-day* science!) The first three chapters in this volume are concerned to show that there is extremely little to this idea. I begin with a look at some of the ways in which philosophers have suggested that modern science explains the link between language and the world. The first chapter discusses the decidedly premature enthusiasm that some philosophers feel for "Artificial Intelligence". The second chapter takes on the idea that evolutionary theory is the key to the phenomenon of representation, while the third chapter subjects to close scrutiny a contemporary philosopher's claim that one can define reference in terms of causality. I try to show that these ideas lack scientific and philosophical substance, while gaining prestige from the general philosophical climate of deference to the supposed metaphysical significance of science.

Perhaps the most impressive case for the view that one *should* look to present-day science, and especially to physics, for at least a very good sketch of an adequate metaphysics has been made by the British philosopher Bernard Williams, and after a chapter which deals with some of the problems faced by both relativistic and materialistic metaphysicians, I devote a chapter to a close examination of his views.

Not all present-day philosophers are overawed by science,

however, and some of the philosophers who are not—philosophers like Derrida, or, in the English-speaking world, Nelson Goodman or Richard Rorty—have reacted to the difficulty of making sense of our cognitive relation to the world by denying that we do have a cognitive relation to extralinguistic reality. In my sixth chapter, I criticize these thinkers for throwing away the baby with the bathwater. In the seventh and eighth chapters, I examine Wittgenstein's "Lectures on Religious Belief", arguing that those lectures demonstrate how a philosopher can lead us to see our various forms of life differently without being either scientistic or irresponsibly metaphysical, while in the concluding chapter I try to show how John Dewey's political philosophy exhibits the same possibility in a very different way.

The two months that I spent at St. Andrews giving these lectures were a sheer delight, and I profited more than I can say from the companionship and the philosophical conversation of the remarkable group of brilliant and dedicated philosophers there, particularly Peter Clark, Bob Hale, John Haldane, Stephen Read, Leslie Stevenson, John Skorupski, and Crispin Wright. As always in recent years, many of the ideas in these chapters were first tried out in conversation with Jim Conant, and Chapter 5, in particular, owes a great deal to those conversations. Chapter 9 first appeared, in a slightly different form, in *Southern California Law Review* 63 (1990): 1671–97, and is reprinted here with that journal's permission. I am also grateful to Bengt Molander of the University of Uppsala and to Ben-Ami Sharfstein of the University of Tel Aviv, both of whom read earlier versions and made valuable suggestions. At a very late stage, excellent suggestions were also made by the referees for the Harvard University Press, not all of which I could take up without changing the character of the work, but some of which I have responded to, and some of which will show their effect in my future writing. The most valuable suggestions of all were made by Ruth Anna Putnam, who provided not only the affection and support which mean so much, but whose close reading and fine criticism certainly made this a much better book.

RENEWING PHILOSOPHY

1

The Project of Artificial Intelligence

Traditionally Gifford Lectures have dealt with questions connected with religion. In recent years, although reference to religion has never been wholly absent, they have sometimes been given by scientists and philosophers of science, and have dealt with the latest knowledge in cosmology, elementary particle physics, and so on. No doubt the change reflects a change in the culture, and particularly in the philosophical culture. But these facts about the Gifford Lectures—their historical concern with religion and their more recent concern with science—both speak to me. As a practicing Jew, I am someone for whom the religious dimension of life has become increasingly important, although it is not a dimension that I know how to philosophize about except by indirection; and the study of science has loomed large in my life. In fact, when I first began to teach philosophy, back in the early 1950s, I thought of myself as a philosopher of science (although I included philosophy of language and philosophy of mind in my generous interpretation of the phrase "philosophy of science"). Those who know my writings from that period may wonder how I reconciled my religious streak, which existed to some extent even back then, and my general scientific materialist worldview at that time. The answer is that I didn't reconcile them. I was a thoroughgoing atheist, and I was a believer. I simply kept these two parts of myself separate.

In the main, however, it was the scientific materialist that was dominant in me in the fifties and sixties. I believed that everything there is can be explained and described by a single theory. Of course we shall never know that theory in detail, and even about the general principles we shall always be somewhat in error. But I believed that we can see in present-day science what the general outlines of such a theory must look like. In particular, I believed that the best metaphysics is physics, or, more precisely, that the best metaphysics is what the positivists called "unified science", science pictured as based on and unified by the application of the laws of fundamental physics. In our time, Bernard Williams has claimed that we have at least a sketch of an "absolute conception of the world" in present-day physics.[1] Many analytic philosophers today subscribe to such a view, and for a philosopher who subscribes to it the task of philosophy becomes largely one of commenting on and speculating about the progress of science, especially as it bears or seems to bear on the various traditional problems of philosophy.

When I was young, a very different conception of philosophy was represented by the work of John Dewey. Dewey held that the idea of a single theory that explains everything has been a disaster in the history of philosophy. Science itself, Dewey once pointed out, has never consisted of a single unified theory, nor have the various theories which existed at any one time ever been wholly consistent. While we should not stop trying to make our theories consistent—Dewey did not regard inconsistency as a *virtue*—in philosophy we should abandon the dream of a single absolute conception of the world, he thought. Instead of seeking a final theory—whether it calls itself an "absolute conception of the world" or not—that would explain everything, we should see philosophy as a reflection on how human beings can resolve the various sorts of "problematical situations" that they encounter, whether in science, in ethics, in politics, in education, or wherever. My own philosophical evolution has been from a view like Bernard Williams' to a view much more like John Dewey's. In this book I want to explain and, to the extent possible in the space available, to justify this change in my philosophical attitude.

In the first three chapters, I begin with a look at some of the ways in which philosophers have suggested that modern cognitive science explains the the link between language and the world. This chapter deals with Artificial Intelligence. Chapter 2 will discuss the idea that evolutionary theory is the key to the mysteries of intentionality (i.e., of truth and reference), while Chapter 3 will discuss the claim made by the philosopher Jerry Fodor that one can define reference in terms of causal/counterfactual notions. In particular, I want to suggest that we can and should accept the idea that cognitive psychology does not simply reduce to brain science *cum* computer science, in the way that so many people (including most practitioners of "cognitive science") expect it to.

I just spoke of a particular picture of what the scientific worldview is, the view that science ultimately reduces to physics, or at least is unified by the world picture of physics. The idea of the mind as a sort of "reckoning machine" goes back to the birth of that "scientific worldview" in the seventeenth and eighteenth centuries. For example, Hobbes suggested that thinking is appropriately called "reckoning", because it really is a manipulation of signs according to rules (analogous to calculating rules), and La Mettrie scandalized his time with the claim that man is just a machine *(L'Homme Machine)*.[2] These ideas were, not surprisingly, associated with materialism. And the question which anyone who touches on the topic of Artificial Intelligence is asked again and again is "Do you think that a computing machine could have intelligence, consciousness, and so on, in the way that human beings do?" Sometimes the question is meant as "could it in principle" and sometimes as "could it really, in practice" (to my mind, the far more interesting question).

The story of the computer, and of Alan Turing's role in the conception of the modern computer, has often been told. In the thirties, Turing formulated the notion of computability[3] in terms which connect directly with computers (which had not yet been invented). In fact, the modern digital computer is a realization of the idea of a "universal Turing machine". A couple of decades later materialists like my former self came to claim that "the mind is a Turing machine". It is interesting to ask why this seemed so evident to me (and still seems evident to many philosophers of mind).

If the whole human body is a physical system obeying the laws of Newtonian physics, and if any such system, up to and including the whole physical universe, is at least metaphorically a machine, then the whole human body is at least metaphorically a machine. And materialists believe that a human being *is* just a living human body. So, as long as they assume that quantum mechanics cannot be relevant to the philosophy of mind (as I did when I made this suggestion),[4] materialists are committed to the view that a human being is—at least metaphorically—a machine. It is understandable that the notion of a Turing machine might be seen as just a way of making this materialist idea precise. Understandable, but hardly well thought out.

The problem is the following: a "machine" in the sense of a physical system obeying the laws of Newtonian physics need not be a Turing machine. (In defense of my former views, I should say that this was not known in the early 1960s when I proposed my so-called functionalist account of mind.) For a Turing machine can compute a function only if that function belongs to a certain class of functions, the so-called general recursive functions. But it has been proved that there exist possible physical systems whose time evolution is not describable by a recursive function, even when the initial condition of the system is so describable. (The wave equation of classical physics has been shown to give rise to examples.) In less technical language, what this means is that there exist physically possible analogue devices which can "compute" non-recursive functions.[5] Even if such devices cannot actually be prepared by a physicist (and Georg Kreisel has pointed out that no theorem has been proved *excluding* the preparation of such a device),[6] it does not follow that they do not occur in nature. Moreover, there is no reason at all why the real numbers describing the condition at a specified time of a naturally occurring physical system should be "recursive". So, for more than one reason, a naturally occurring physical system might well have a trajectory which "computed" a non-recursive function.

You may wonder, then, why I assumed that a human being could be, at least as a reasonable idealization, regarded as a Turing machine. One reason was that the following bit of reasoning occurred to me. A human being cannot live forever. A human being is finite in space and time. And the words and actions—the "outputs", in computer jargon—of a human being, insofar as they are perceivable by the unaided senses of other human beings (and we might plausibly assume that this is the level of accuracy aimed at in cognitive psychology) can be described by physical parameters which are specified to only a certain macroscopic level of accuracy. But this means that the "outputs" can be predicted during the finite time the human lives by a sufficiently good approximation to the actual continuous trajectory, and such a "sufficiently good approximation" can be a recursive function. (Any function can be approximated to any fixed level of accuracy by a recursive function over any finite time interval.) Since we may assume that the possible values of the boundary parameters are also restricted to a finite range, a finite set of such recursive functions will give the behavior of the human being under all possible conditions in the specified range to the desired accuracy. (Since the laws of motion are continuous, the boundary conditions need only to be known to within some appropriate Δ in order to predict the trajectory of the system to within the specified accuracy.) But if that is the case, the "outputs"—what the human says and does—can be predicted by a Turing machine. (In fact, the Turing machine only has to compute the values of whichever recursive function in the finite set corresponds to the values that the boundary conditions have taken on), and such a Turing machine could, in principle, simulate the behavior in question as well as predict it.

This argument proves too much and too little, however. On the one hand, it proves that *every* physical system whose behavior we want to know only up to some specified level of accuracy and whose "lifetime" is finite can be simulated by an automaton! But it does not prove that such a simulation is in any sense a *perspicuous representation* of the behavior of the system. When an airplane is flying through the air at less than supersonic speeds, it is perspicuous to represent the air as a continuous liquid, and *not* as an automaton. On the other hand it proves too little from the point of view of those who want to say that the real value of computational models is that they show what our "competence" is in idealization from such limitations as the finiteness of our memory or our lifetimes. According to such thinkers,[7] *if we were able to live forever, and were allowed access to a potentially infinite memory storage, still all our linguistic behavior could be simulated by an automaton.* We are best "idealized" as Turing machines, such thinkers say, when what is at stake is not our actual "performance" but our "competence". Since the proof of the little theorem I just demonstrated depended *essentially* on assuming that we do not live forever and on assuming that the boundary conditions have a finite range (which excludes a potentially infinite external memory), it offers no comfort to such a point of view.

Again, it might be said that any non-recursivities either in our initial conditions or in our space-time trajectories could not be reliably detected and hence would have no "cognitive" significance. But it is one thing to claim that the *particular* non-recursive function a human might compute if the human (under a certain idealization) were allowed to live forever has no cognitive significance, and another to say that the whole infinite trajectory can *therefore* be approximated by a Turing machine. Needless to say, what follows the "therefore" in this last sentence does not follow logically from the antecedent! (Recall how in the "chaos" phenomena small perturbations become magnified in the course of time.)

In sum, it does not seem that there is any principled reason why we must be perspicuously representable as Turing machines, *even assuming the truth of materialism*. (Or any reason why we must be representable in this way at all—even non-perspicuously—under the idealization that we live forever and have potentially infinite external memories). That is all I shall say about the question whether we are (or can be represented as) Turing machines "in principle".

On the other hand, the interesting question *is* precisely whether we are perspicuously representable as Turing machines, even if there are no a priori answers to be had to this question. And this is something that can be found out only by seeing if we can "simulate" human intelligence *in practice*. Accordingly, it is to this question that I now turn.

Induction and Artificial Intelligence

A central part of human intelligence is the ability to make inductive inferences, that is, to learn from experience. In the case of deductive logic, we have discovered a set of rules which satisfactorily formalize valid inference. In the case of inductive logic this has not so far proved possible, and it is worthwhile pausing to ask why.

In the first place, it is not clear just how large the scope of inductive logic is supposed to be. Some writers consider the "hypothetico-deductive method"—that is, the inference from the success of a theory's predictions to the acceptability of the theory—the most important part of inductive logic, while others regard it as already belonging to a different subject. Of course, if by induction we mean "any method of valid inference which is not deductive", then the scope of the topic of inductive logic will be simply enormous.

If the success of a large number of predictions—say, a thousand, or ten thousand—which are not themselves consequences of the auxiliary hypotheses alone *always* confirmed a theory, then the hypothetico-deductive inference, at least, would be easy to formalize. But problems arise at once. Some theories are accepted when the number of confirmed predictions is still very small—this was the case with the general theory of relativity, for example. To take care of such cases, we postulate that it is not only the number of confirmed predictions that matters, but also the elegance or simplicity of the theory: but can such quasi-aesthetic notions as "elegance" and "simplicity" really be formalized? Formal measures have indeed been proposed, but it cannot be said that they shed any light on real-life scientific inference. Moreover, a confirmed theory sometimes fits badly with background knowledge; in some cases, we conclude the theory cannot be true, while in others we conclude that the background knowledge should be modified; again, apart from imprecise talk about "simplicity", it is hard to say what determines whether it is better, in a concrete case, to preserve background knowledge or to modify it. And even a theory which leads to a vast number of successful predictions may not be accepted if someone points out that a much simpler theory would lead to those predictions as well.

In view of these difficulties, some students of inductive logic would confine the scope of the subject to simpler inferences—typically, to the inference from the statistics in a sample drawn from a population to the statistics in the population. When the population consists of objects which exist at different times, including future times, the present sample is never going to be a random selection from the whole population, however; so the key case is this: I have a sample which is a random selection from the members of a population which exist *now, here* (on Earth, in Scotland, in the particular place where I have been able to gather samples, or wherever); what can I conclude about the properties of *future* members of the population (and of members in other places)?

If the sample is a sample of uranium atoms, and the future members are in the near as opposed to the cosmological future, then we are prepared to believe that the future members will resemble present members, on the average. If the sample is a sample of people, and the future members of the population are not in the very near future, then we are less likely to make this assumption, at least if culturally variable traits are in question. Here we are guided by background knowledge, of course. This has suggested to some inquirers that perhaps all there is to induction is the skilful use of background knowledge—we just "bootstrap" our way from what we know to additional knowledge. But then the cases in which we don't have much background knowledge at all, as well as the exceptional cases in which what we have to do is *question* background knowledge, assume great importance; and here, as just remarked, no one has much to say beyond vague talk about "simplicity".

The problem of induction is not by any means the only problem confronting anyone who seriously intends to simulate human intelligence. Induction, indeed all cognition, presupposes the ability to recognize similarities among things; but similarities are by no means just constancies of the physical stimulus, or simple patterns in the input to the sense organs. For this reason, the success certain computer programs have had in detecting patterns (e.g., the shapes of letters of the alphabet) does not solve the "similarity" problem in the form in which it confronts someone learning a natural language. What makes knives similar, for example, is not that they all look alike (they don't), but that they are all manufactured to cut or stab;[8] any system that can recognize knives as relevantly similar needs to be able to attribute purposes to agents. Humans have no difficulty in doing this; but it is not clear that we do this by unaided induction; we may well have a "hard-wired-in" ability to "put ourselves in the shoes" of other people which enables us to attribute to them any purposes we are capable of attributing to ourselves—an ability that Evolution the Tinker found it convenient to endow us with, and which helps us to know which of the infinitely many possible inductions we might consider is likely to be successful. Again, to recognize that a chihuahua and a Great Dane are similar in the sense of belonging to the same species requires the ability to realize that, appearances notwithstanding,[9] chihuahuas can impregnate Great Danes and produce fertile offspring. Thinking in terms of potential for mating and potential for reproduction is natural for us; but it need not be natural for an *artificial* intelligence—unless we deliberately simulate this human propensity when we construct the artificial intelligence. Such examples can be multiplied indefinitely.

Similarities expressed by adjectives and verbs rather than nouns can be even more complex. A non-human "intelligence" might know what white is on a color chart, for example, without being able to see why pinko-grey humans are called "white", and it might know what it is to open a door without being able to understand why we speak of opening a border (or opening trade). There are many words (as Wittgenstein pointed out) that apply to things that have only a "family resemblance" to one another; there need not be one thing all X's have in common. For example, we speak of the Canaanite tribal chiefs mentioned in the bible as kings although their kingdoms were probably little more than villages, and we speak of George VI (who did not literally rule England at all) as a king; and there are even cases in history in which "the kingship was not hereditary", we say. Similarly (Wittgenstein's example), there is no property all games have in common which distinguishes them from all the activities which are not games.

The notional task of artificial intelligence is to simulate intelligence, not to duplicate it. So, perhaps one might finesse the problems I just mentioned by constructing a system that reasoned in an ideal language[10]—one in which words did not change their extensions in a context-dependent way (a sheet of typing paper might be "$white_1$" and a human being might be "$white_2$", in such a language, where $white_1$ is color-chart white, and $white_2$ is pinko-grey). Perhaps all "family resemblance" words would have to be barred from such a language. (How much of a vocabulary would be left?) But my budget of difficulties is not yet finished.

Because the project of symbolic inductive logic appeared to run out of steam after Carnap, the thinking among philosophers of science has run in the direction of talking about so-called bootstrapping methods—that is, methods which attribute a great deal to background knowledge. It is instructive to see why this has happened, and also to realize how unsatisfactory such an approach is if our aim is to simulate intelligence.

One huge problem might be described as the existence of *conflicting inductions*. To use an example from Nelson Goodman:[11] as far as I know, no one who has ever entered Emerson Hall in Harvard University has been able to speak Inuit (Eskimo). Thinking formalistically, this suggests the induction that if any person X enters Emerson Hall, then X does not speak Inuit. Let Ukuk be an Eskimo in Alaska who speaks Inuit. Shall I predict that if Ukuk enters Emerson Hall, then Ukuk will no longer be able to speak Inuit? Obviously not, but what is wrong with this induction?

Goodman answers that what is wrong with the inference is that it conflicts with the "better entrenched" inductively supported law that people do not lose their ability to speak a language upon entering a new place. But how am I supposed to know that this law *does* have more confirming instances than the regularity that no one who enters Emerson Hall speaks Inuit? Background knowledge again?

As a matter of fact, I don't believe that as a child I had any idea how often either of the conflicting regularities in the example (conflicting in that one of them must fail if Ukuk enters Emerson Hall) had been confirmed, but I would still have known enough not to make the "silly" induction that Ukuk would stop being able to speak Inuit if he entered a building (or a country) where no one had spoken Inuit. Again it is not clear that the knowledge that one doesn't lose a language just like that *is* really the product of induction—perhaps this is something we have an innate propensity to believe or, if that seems unreasonable, something that we have an innate propensity to conclude on the basis of only a little experience. The question that won't go away is *how much what we call "intelligence" presupposes the rest of human nature.*

Moreover, if what matters really is "entrenchment" (that is, number and variety of confirming instances), and if the information that the universal statement "one doesn't lose one's ability to speak a language upon entering a new place" is better entrenched than the universal statement "no one who enters Emerson Hall speaks Inuit" is part of my background knowledge, it isn't clear how it got there. Perhaps this information is implicit in the way people speak about linguistic abilities; but then one is faced with the question of how one "decodes" the implicit information conveyed by the utterances one hears.

The problem of conflicting inductions is a ubiquitous one even if one restricts attention to the simplest inductive inferences. If the solution is really just to give the system more background knowledge, then what are the implications for Artificial Intelligence? It is not easy to say, because Artificial Intelligence as we know it doesn't really try to simulate intelligence at all; simulating intelligence is only its notional activity, while its real activity is just writing clever programs for a variety of tasks. This is an important and useful activity, although, of course, it does not sound as exciting as "simulating human intelligence" or "producing artificial intelligence". But if Artificial Intelligence existed as a real rather than a notional research activity, there would be two alternative strategies its practitioners could follow in the face of the problem of background knowledge.

(1) One could simply try to program into the machine *all* of the information a sophisticated human inductive judge has (including the tacit information). At the least it would require generations of researchers to formalize this information (probably it could not be done at all, because of the sheer quantity

of information involved); and it is not clear that the result would be more than a gigantic "expert system". No one would find this very exciting; and such an "intelligence" would be dreadfully unimaginative, unable to realize that in many cases it is precisely background knowledge that needs to be given up.

(2) One could undertake the more exciting and ambitious task of constructing a device that could *learn* the background knowledge by interacting with human beings, as a child learns a language and all the cultural information, explicit and tacit, that comes with growing up in a human community.

The Natural Language Problem

The second alternative is certainly the project that deserves the name of Artificial Intelligence. But consider the problems: to figure out the information implicit in the things people say, the machine must simulate "understanding" a human language. Thus the idea mentioned above, of sticking to an artificial "ideal language" and ignoring the complexities of natural language, has to be abandoned if this strategy is adopted; abandoned because the cost is too high. Too much of the information the machine would need is retrievable only via natural language processing.

But the natural language problem presents many of the same difficulties all over again. Some thinkers—Chomsky and his school—believe that a "template" for natural language, including the semantic or conceptual aspects, is innate—hard-wired-in by Evolution the Tinker. Although this view is taken to extremes by Fodor, who holds that there is an innate language of thought, with primitives adequate for the expression of all concepts that humans are able to learn to express in a natural language, Chomsky himself has hesitated to go this far: it seems that what he is committed to is the existence of a large number of innate conceptual abilities which give us a propensity to form certain concepts and not others. (In conversation, he has suggested that the difference between postulating innate concepts and innate abilities is not important if the postulated abilities are sufficiently structured.) At the opposite extreme, there is the view of classical behaviorism, which sought to explain language learning as a special case of the application of general rules for acquiring "habits"—i.e., as just one more bundle of inductions. (An in-between position is, of course, possible: why should language learning not depend partly on special-purpose heuristics and partly on general learning strategies—both developed by evolution?)

The view that language learning is not really learning, but rather the maturation of an innate ability in a particular environment (somewhat like the acquisition of a bird call by a species of bird that has to hear the call from an adult bird of the species to acquire it, but which also has an innate propensity to acquire that sort of call) leads, in its extreme form, to pessimism about the likelihood that human use of natural language can be successfully simulated on a computer—which is why Chomsky is pessimistic about projects for natural language computer processing, although he shares the computer model of the brain, or at least of the "language organ", with AI researchers. Notice that this pessimistic view of language learning parallels the pessimistic view that induction is not a single ability, but rather a manifestation of a complex human nature whose computer simulation would require a vast system of subroutines—so vast that generations of researchers would be required to formalize even a small part of the system. Similarly, the optimistic view that there is an algorithm (of manageable size) for inductive logic is paralleled by the optimistic view of language learning: that there is a more or less topic-neutral heuristic for learning, and that this heuristic suffices (without the aid of an unmanageably large stock of hard-wired-in background knowledge, or topic-specific conceptual abilities) for the learning of one's natural language, as well as for the making of inductive inferences in general. Perhaps the optimistic view is right; but I do not see anyone on the scene, in either Artificial Intelligence or inductive logic, who has any interesting ideas as to how the topic-neutral learning strategy *works*.

The Mind as Chaos

When I published a paper with these arguments,[12] the American philosopher Daniel Dennett[13] characterized my view as "the mind as chaos." This is an interesting charge.

Up to now I have been discussing the prospects of simulating human intelligence, not the prospects of finding informative models of the way the brain works. Dennett is connecting the two tasks: in effect, he is claiming that pessimism about the success of AI in simulating human intelligence amounts to pessimism about the possibility of describing the functioning of the brain. Hidden in this charge is a variant of Pascal's wager: you have nothing to lose if you assume AI will succeed and you are wrong, but if you assume AI will not succeed, you will lose the only chance there is to describe the brain. But what connection is there between simulating intelligence and describing the brain?

Even if the computer model of the brain is correct, it does not at all follow that AI will succeed. As mentioned above, Noam Chomsky believes the computer model is correct, but he does not expect AI to succeed. Language-using, he once put it to me in conversation, is not a *separable* ability of human beings: you can simulate baseball-throwing without simulating total human intellectual capacity, but you cannot simulate language-using—even language-using in a fixed context, such as going to the store and buying some milk, without simulating total human intellectual capacity. Yet Chomsky does not despair of understanding the brain; we can understand the weather without being able to predict it any better than we could before, and we may understand the brain, as a hierarchically structured system of computational systems ("modules"), without being able to describe all of them and all of their interactions well enough to predict or even simulate the brain's activities.

Another example which makes the same point is the current interest in computer models of the brain which do not assume that the brain computes using "representations" and rules for manipulating those representations in the style of a logical calculus.[14] Perhaps the most interesting of these is the "neural Darwinist" model suggested by Gerald Edelman.[15] Knowing that such a model of the brain was correct would not, in and of itself, enable us to predict which inductions the person whose brain that was would make; that depends on the system(s) of hard-wired-in basic similarities, and (in the "neural Darwinist" model, on the operation of an analogue to natural selection in the unique individual brain) there may be a vast number of such systems (and selection events) at different levels of the brain's processing activity. Yet, if we verified that such a model was correct, we would hardly express the discovery by saying "the mind has turned out to be chaos". And the same thing goes if we discover that some model that does *not* come from computer science at all is the best model for the brain's activity. Many systems are too complex for us to survey and predict or simulate their activity in detail; this is not to say that we cannot seek useful theoretical models of such systems. To take an example from a totally different field, pessimism about the possibility of ever realistically simulating the behavior of an economy over a reasonably long period of time is not the same thing as pessimism about the possibility of a science of economics.

There is another side to Dennett's charge that I think the mind is chaos, however. Dennett is saying—and Fodor often says[16]—that pessimism about the power of computational models is scepticism about the possibility of "cognitive science". But the hidden premise in both thinkers' minds is a reductionist one. There is, in fact, an enormous amount of cognitive psychology that is not at all reductionist. There is no reason why the study of human cognition requires that we try to reduce cognition either to computations or to brain processes. We may very well succeed in discovering theoretical models of the brain which vastly increase our understanding of how the brain works without being of very much help to most areas of psychology, and in discovering better theoretical models in psychology (cognitive and otherwise) which are not of any particular help to brain science. The idea that the only understanding worthy of the name is reductionist understanding is a tired one, but evidently it has not lost its grip on our scientific culture.

2

Does Evolution Explain Representation?

For the last three centuries a certain metaphysical picture suggested by Newtonian or Galilean physics has been repeatedly confused with physics itself. (More recently, metaphysical pictures suggested by biology and by computer science have been confused with those subjects themselves, in much the same way.) Philosophers who love that picture do not have very much incentive to point out the confusion—if a philosophical picture is taken to be *the* picture endorsed by science, then attacks on the picture will seem to be attacks on science, and few philosophers will wish to be seen as enemies of science. As far as our ways of understanding mind and language are concerned, the thrust of that picture was well captured by the claim of La Mettrie that man is a machine.

The discovery of the idea of evolution by natural selection by Darwin and Wallace approximately a hundred years later seemed to add further evidence for the thesis that mind is to be understood by being reduced to physics and chemistry (we know from Darwin's journals that that is how he himself was inclined to see the matter). Today even materialist philosophers do not think that follows; it is on computer modeling, rather than on direct physical or chemical explanation, that thinkers of a reductionist bent, like my former self, now pin their hopes. But recently evolutionary theory has again come into play in discussions of the nature of mind, and of the relation of language to reality.

Philosophers who apply the theory of evolution generally do so in a very simple way. The philosopher picks some capacity that human beings have, a capacity which it is in one way or another useful for human beings to have, and argues that it must have been selected for in the evolutionary process. This use of the theory of evolution is one that many evolutionary biologists find extremely questionable.[1] The working evolutionary biologist does not assume that every useful capacity of a species is the result of selection. A genetic alteration frequently has many different effects. If any one of those effects contributes markedly to the reproductive success of members of the species having that gene, then that new genetic trait will be selected for, and other side effects, provided they are not so negative as to cancel out the benefits of having the new genetic trait, will be carried along. In this way, it can even happen that a trait which does not contribute to the survival potential or the reproductive success of a species, or even one which it would be better for the species not to have, arises through natural selection without itself being selected for. But it can also happen that the trait which is carried along is actually beneficial to the species, although that is not the reason why the trait became universal in the species. In general, the assumption that every change in a species which is beneficial to the species was *specifically* selected for is rejected in contemporary evolutionary theory. Evolutionists are extremely cautious about saying which capacities and organs and so on were specifically selected for (were "adaptations") in the evolutionary history of a species and which ones arose serendipitously. Philosophers, however, are not so cautious.[2]

Evolution, Language, and the World

My primary concern in this chapter is with philosophical views of the mind, and with the way in which philosophical issues about the mind become entangled with various other issues. In a famous letter to Marcus Herz, Kant described the problem of how anything in the mind can be a "representation" of anything outside the mind as the most difficult riddle in philosophy.[3] Since the so-called linguistic turn in philosophy earlier in this century, that question has been replaced by the question "How does language hook onto the world?" but the replacement has not made finding an answer any easier. Recently certain philosophers[4] have suggested that the answer is provided by the theory of natural selection, either directly or indirectly. I want to examine this idea partly for its own intrinsic interest, and partly because it provides a natural transition to questions about the language-world relation. I will first state the idea in a very general way.

Cognitive scientists have frequently suggested in recent years that the brain employs "representations" in processing data and guiding action. Even the simplest pattern-recognizing devices in the brain could be described as producing representations. In his books *Neurobiology* and *The Remembered Present*, Gerald Edelman has described a neural architecture which could enable the brain to construct its own pattern-recognizing devices without "knowing in advance" exactly which patterns it will have to recognize. This architecture will enable a brain to develop a neural assembly which will fire whenever the letter A is presented in the visual field, for example, or alternatively to develop a neural assembly which will fire whenever the Hebrew letter aleph or a Chinese character is presented in the visual field, without having "innate" A-recognizing devices or

aleph-recognizing devices or Chinese-character-recognizing devices. If Edelman's model is right, then when an instance of
the letter A is presented in my visual field and the appropriate
neural assembly fires, that firing could be described as a "representation" of the shape "A". But the representations that neu-
robiologists, linguists, and computer scientists hypothesize go
far beyond mere pattern recognizers.

If an organism is to display what we call intelligence it is obviously useful, and perhaps necessary (as Edelman and others have
suggested), for it to have, or to be able to construct, something
that functions as a map of its environment, with aspects that
represent the various salient features of that environment, such
as food, enemies, and places of refuge. At a higher level, such
a map might be elaborated to show not only salient features of
the current environment, but also a representation of the creature itself, and perhaps even a representation of the creature's
psychological states ("self-consciousness"). In *The Remembered
Present*, Edelman speculates about the sorts of neural architecture that might support a capacity to develop such representa-
tional schemata. All this is exciting science, or at least exciting
scientific speculation. Whether or not it will pay off is not for
me to judge, but of course I hope that it will. My doubt
concerns whether neural science (or computer science, insofar
as it leads to an increase in our ability to model the brain) can
really speak to the philosophical question that I mentioned.

What philosophers want to know is what representation is.
They are concerned with discovering the "nature" of representation. To discover that, in addition to the representations we
are all acquainted with—thoughts, words, and sentences—there
are other things which don't look like thoughts or words, things
in the brain which it is useful to analogize to representations,
is not to tell us what representation is. If a philosopher asks
what the nature of representation is, and one tells him or her

that there are tens of millions of representations in the Widener Library, one has not answered the question. And if one tells him or her that there are tens of millions of representations in human brains, one has not answered the question either. Or so it would seem.

Let us take the form of the philosopher's question that I mentioned a few moments ago, "How does language hook onto the world?" Materialist philosophers generally favor one of two answers to this question. One kind of answer, which I shall not discuss here, uses notions from information theory. That answer has, however, run into apparently insuperable technical difficulties.[5] The other answer, which is today the favorite one among philosophical materialists, is that in the case of language, reference is a matter of "causal connection". The problem is to spell out the details, and in the next chapter I will examine one attempt to do this. Even before we look at such an attempt, it is apparent from the very beginning that there are going to be difficulties with the details—whether those difficulties prove insuperable or not. One cannot simply say that the word "cat" refers to cats because the word is causally connected to cats, for the word "cat", or rather my way of using the word "cat", is causally connected to many things. It is true that I wouldn't be using the word "cat" as I do if there were no cats; my causal history, or the causal history of others from whom I learned the language, involved interactions with cats; but I also wouldn't be using the word "cat" as I do if many other things were different. My present use of the word "cat" has a great many causes, not just one. The use of the word "cat" is causally connected to cats, but it is also causally connected to the behavior of Anglo-Saxon tribes, for example. Just mentioning "causal connection" does not explain how one thing can be a representation of another thing, as Kant was already aware.

For this reason, philosophers who offer this sort of account do not try to account for all forms of representation—that is too big a project to carry through at one fell swoop—but to account for forms of representation that might be thought basic, that is, for representation of observable objects in our immediate environment, such as trees and people and animals and tables and chairs.

It is natural to suppose that the ability to represent such objects is the result of natural selection. My ability to understand the word "cat", for example, might involve my connecting that word with a more primitive representation of cats, a representation that is not itself a part of a language. It may be that in my representation of my environment, there is some "data structure" which "stands for" cats. To say that it stands for cats—this is the crucial move—is simply to say that an acccount of the evolutionary function of that data structure, and of the schematism to which that data structure belongs, will involve saying that that data structure enables us to survive and to reproduce our genes, or the entire schematism enables us to survive and reproduce our genes, because various parts of that schematism, including the data structure, have the "function" of corresponding to various things and kinds of things in the environment. Having the function of corresponding to things and kinds of things in that way just *is* representation, or rather, it is what we might call "primitive representation". If the problem of saying what representation is is not solved, the thought is, then at least progress has been made if this story is right. If this story is right, then we have at least a hope of saying what primitive representation is, and then philosophers can work on the task of showing how the more elaborate notion of representation that we actually possess is related to and grows out of primitive representation.

Let me emphasize that, according to the view I am describing, the intentional notion "stands for" can be *defined* by saying that "A stands for B" (where A is the data structure in the brain and B is the external referent) just means that "A stands to B in a relation (a correspondence, that is, a function from As to Bs) which plays such-and-such-a-role in an evolutionary explanation." "Stands for" is not being taken as primitive, if this works; "evolutionary explanation" *is*.

The way in which I just explained the idea makes it sound as if the notion of a cat is supposed to be innate. While some thinkers—Jerrry Fodor is the best known—would indeed posit that the various data structures that make up the mental schematism that we use to represent our environment are indeed innate, others, like Gerald Edelman, would not. If Edelman's story is right, what is innate is not the mental representations themselves, but only the architecture which permits us to form such representations. While Edelman himself is wary of trying to answer the philosophical question about the nature of reference, someone who takes the line I have described could very well accept Edelman's model. What such a philosopher would have to do is insist that the architecture was selected for *to perform the function* of creating data structures which correspond in a certain way to objects in the environment and to kinds of objects in the environment. And again the claim would be that that correspondence, the correspondence which we have to talk about in explaining how the whole mental schematism came to be as the result of natural selection, is at least the primitive form of reference.[6]

The idea is that natural selection is, so to speak, teleological: it produces things that have a *telos* or a "function", and a structured way of performing that function. We can say what representation is by saying what the structures are that mediate representation, that is, how those structures function to enable the animal to survive and reproduce, and how a correspondence between structures in the head and things outside the head plays a role in that mediation, and then we can eliminate the mystery of teleology by showing how the teleology appears here, as it does, say, in the functioning of the foot or the functioning of the eye, as the result of familiar processes of natural selection.

In what follows, I am going to confine attention to the form of the theory in which the individual representations are themselves innate, but it should be clear how the philosophical arguments should be modified if one takes the other form of the theory.

To begin with, let us consider what it means to say that a trait was selected for. All explanations of selection involve counterfactual conditionals at one point or another. For example, if we say that the speed of the gazelle was selected for, what we will typically mean is something like this: that the gazelle needs to escape from certain predators, for instance from lions, if it is to survive and have offspring; and that the gazelles with a certain genotype, the one responsible for higher speed, lived to have offspring in greater numbers; and finally—we have to add—that they *would not have* survived in greater numbers *if they had not* run so fast: the lions would have caught them. This last addition is necessary, because without this addition the possibility is not ruled out that the genotype that is responsible for higher speed was selected for for some reason other than the higher speed that accompanies its presence.

If the gazelles had not run so fast, the lions would have caught them. This sentence, and others like it, "do the work" in powering explanations by natural selection. That an explanation by natural selection involves the use of counterfactuals is not a difficulty from the point of view of the philosophers I am talking about, since they are all committed to using counterfactuals, dispositional statements, and so on in the analysis of reference.

There are, indeed, philosophers who regard counterfactuals as being just as problematic as reference itself—not to mention those, like Quine and Goodman, who regard counterfactuals as *more* problematic than reference itself—but this is an issue I have to defer to later chapters.

The sense in which the gazelles' high speed is there for a purpose, the sense in which it has a "function", is really rather minimal, which is why Ernst Mayr has proposed that we should speak not of teleology in evolutionary theory, but of teleology-simulation, or, as he puts it, "teleonomy".[7] Escaping lions is the function of the genetic trait in question only in the sense that if the high speed had not enabled the gazelles to escape the lions, then that feature would not have been selected for. *converse?*

Now, let us suppose that there are innate mental representations in the case of a certain species, say the dog. Let us suppose that one of the innate representations in the dog's brain is the representation of meat. What this will mean should be clear: we are saying that the dog's mental processes involve a "data structure" which was selected for to do certain things; perhaps the data structure responds in a certain way when the dog sees meat, and this somehow triggers the appropriate responses, such as trying to get it, and eating it. Perhaps the data structure also operates in yet another way: when the dog wants meat, the data structure causes the dog to seek meat, or to whine to be fed, or whatever. Whatever the details may be, the point is that there are certain behaviors which involve meat and which involve the data structure, and the architecture which makes it possible for the data structure to mediate the behavior in that way was selected for. Again, any reference to teleology is unnecessary; all it means to say that this architecture was selected for this purpose is that if having a data structure which triggers these behaviors under these conditions had not enabled the dog to get food more often, then the dog would not have survived to reproduce its genes more often than other dogs with different genes. The important point (if some story like this one proves to be correct) is that the *explanation* of how the data structure came to be universal among dogs involves a certain "correspondence" between the data structure and meat.

Intentionality and Lower Animals

One difficulty in evaluating the importance of these ideas is that we are all too ready to apply intentional predicates to lower animals in an unreflective way. We all say things like "the dog is trying to reach the meat", and we often seem to think that such descriptions mean that the dog has the propositional attitude of "thinking that what it sees is meat" just as they normally would if we were talking about a fully competent speaker of a natural language. Forget for the moment all evolutionary questions, and suppose we ask whether the dog really thinks that it is *meat* that it sees and reaches for, as opposed to stuff with a certain look and taste and edibility and so forth. Suppose we perform the following experiment: We make a "steak" out of textured vegetable protein. Let us suppose that our technology is so good that the TVP "steak" smells like real steak, looks like real steak, tastes like real steak, and so on. If one sees such a steak, one may well think, "I see a piece of meat". If one eats it, one may be perfectly happy. But if one is told that what one ate was textured vegetable protein, one will revise one's judgment, and decide that one didn't really eat a piece of meat, one ate a piece of TVP. (My oldest child, Erika, started distinguishing between "real" things and "make-believe" things—the beginning of the distinction between appearance and reality— at about the age of two-and-a-half, by the way. I think that the appearance of this distinction between the "real" thing and the "unreal" thing is one of the most exciting developments of a child's language.) Now suppose that we give the synthetic steak to the dog. The dog eats the synthetic steak and is perfectly happy. Did the dog have a false belief? That is, did the dog believe that it saw real meat, just as we believed that we saw real meat, and not know that we had a false belief? Or did the dog's concept of meat include TVP "steaks" to begin with?

The question makes no sense. A speaker of a language can decide that part of his or her concept of meat is that it should come from an animal, for example. A more sophisticated speaker can decide that it is part of the concept of meat that it should have the normal microstructure, whatever that may be. There is probably nothing in the dog's neural architecture which would allow it to think "this piece of meat came from an animal", and there is certainly nothing which would allow it to think "this piece of meat has a normal microstructure".

To illustrate the same point in another way: Suppose we interpret the dog's concept, or as I would prefer to say, its "proto-concept", as referring not to meat but to whatever has a certain appearance and smell and taste. If the "meat" the dog ate on a certain occasion were not really a piece of meat, but a bit of ectoplasm which has been magically endowed with the right smell and taste and texture and appearance, the dog's thought that this is meat would be *true* of what it ate, on this interpretation, for its thought is not about meat in *our* sense, but only about the appropriate smell and taste and texture and appearance. Once again, a human being who discovered that what had just been eaten was not meat, and indeed not even a piece of matter, but a piece of ectoplasm, would take back the judgment that he or she had eaten meat. But the dog lacks the conceptual resources to make such a discovery. To deploy

verificationism?
connection?

the jargon of philosophers of language, assuming dogs have proto-concepts, the dog's proto-concept of meat is "referentially indeterminate" in ways in which human concepts are not. Human concepts are less indeterminate because they enter into complex sentences, and human beings can say whether they believe or disbelieve those various sentences. In the case of the dog, those sentences are missing—sentences like "this meat has a normal molecular structure", "this meat came from an animal", "this meat is matter and not ectoplasm", and all the rest. But even the philosopher of language's way of putting the matter seems to me not radical enough.

The real point is this: human beings are reflective creatures. Human beings are able to think about their own practice, and to criticize it from a number of points of view. If I have a thought and act on it, I can later ask whether my thought was successful or not, whether it achieved its goal, whether it contributed to my well-being, my satisfaction, and so on; but I can also ask whether my thought was true or not, and this is not the same question. I may decide that one of my thoughts was successful in enabling me to maximize my well-being, but was not in fact true. I was deceived, but the deception was a fortunate one.[8] No such cognitive performance is possible in the case of the dog. For a dog, the very distinction between having a true belief and having a successful belief simply does not make sense; and that means that the notion of a dog's thought as being true or false, and of its proto-concepts as referring or not referring to something, simply do not make sense. A dog can recognize that something is illusory only in the sense of encountering a disappointment. If something looks and smells like meat, but turns out to be made of rubber, then when the dog tries to chew it, it will experience disappointment. But the idea that even a successful encounter with "meat" may have succeeded although the belief was *false* is inapplicable in the case of a dog. Evolution didn't "design" dogs' ideas to be true or false, it designed them to be successful or unsuccesful.

Evolution Again   *is the idea of truth a ~~su~~ one of success, too?*

With this "indeterminacy" of the dog's proto-concepts in mind, let us return to the evolutionary story. I postulated that if a certain data structure in the dog's brain (a proto-concept) didn't usually fire when the dog perceived meat, then dogs with a certain genotype wouldn't have survived to have offspring in greater frequency than did dogs with competing genotypes, as they in fact did. But the whole idea that a unique correspondence between the data structure and meat is involved in this bit of natural selection is an illusion, an artifact of the way we described the situation. We could just as well have said that the data structure was selected for because its action normally signals the presence of something which has a certain smell and taste and appearance and is edible.

To this objection the defender of "evolutionary intentionality" might reply that in fact the apparent indeterminacy if we look only at present-day dogs disappears if we consider evolutionary history. In the evolutionary history of the species, synthetic meat did not exist, for example. So, it might be argued, it would be wrong to regard the dog's proto-concept of meat as including synthetic meat. But it is difficult to see the force of this reply, since canned meat also didn't play any role in the evolutionary history of the dog, yet when a domestic dog sees some meat taken out of a can, the defender of evolutionary intentionality will presumably want to say that the dog thinks that that is meat, and that the dog's thought is true. It is also the case, by the way, that poisoned meat played no role in the selection process, since the dogs that ate poisoned meat did not survive to have offspring. Yet those who would take the dog's but TVP wouldn't be one, in the dog's def. of meat, if wouldn't contribute to success

isn't the whole point that reference doesn't matter to the dog?

proto-concept to refer to meat would presumably say of the dog who sees and eats poisoned meat that it was right in thinking that what it saw was meat (although it didn't know the meat was poisoned), and not that what its proto-concept refers to is "unpoisoned meat". Yet, on the evolutionary story, why should one not say that the dog's concept of meat (and the human one too?) refers not to meat but to unpoisoned meat? Alternatively, why should one not just as well say that when the dog is given synthetic meat (or even poisoned meat) the dog thinks that that is "meat-stuff" (where the concept of meat-stuff is wide enough to include synthetic meat) and that the dog's thought is true; or why shouldn't one say that the dog's thought is "that's that great stuff with such and such an appearance and such and such a taste", and that the dog's thought is true? Or, better, why shouldn't one just give up on talk of truth in connection with the thought of lower animals? Perhaps, if one wants to speculate, all that goes on is that certain "mental phenomena" are associated with a feeling that a certain behavior is called for.

Isn't it with dogs as with gazelles? Dogs which tended to eat meat rather than vegetables when both were available produced more offspring (gazelles which ran faster than lions escaped the lions and were thus able to produce more offspring). Just as we aren't tempted to say that gazelles have a proto-concept of running fast, so dogs don't have a proto-concept of meat. Indeed, in the case of the dog, there are a variety of different descriptions of the adaptive behavior: that certain dogs recognize meat better, or that certain dogs recognize food with a certain appearance and taste better, or just that certain dogs just recognize stuff with a certain appearance and taste better. The "reference" we get out of this bit of hypothetical natural selection will be just the reference we put in our choice of a description. Evolution won't give you more intentionality than you pack into it.[9]

Reference and Counterfactuals

The most telling argument against the idea that evolution explains intentionality is that the whole reference to evolution plays no real role in the "explanation" just sketched. What *seems* to give us an account is not the theory of evolution, but the use of counterfactuals and the appeal to considerations of selective reproduction of certain functions. But both of these strategies are available to any philosopher of language, and they require no particular reference to the theory of evolution. For example, a philosopher of language might very well take the following sorts of sentences as basic, at least in an initial investigation of reference: "I see an X", "I am touching an X", "I want an X", and so on. He or she might now say that when X is the name of a kind of observable thing, say a cat or dog, the way these sentences are "connected to the world" is the following: I would not normally assert that I see a cat, or I am touching a cat, or I want a cat unless I were (respectively) seeing a cat, or touching a cat, or wanting a cat. These claims are certainly correct. I wouldn't, in fact, normally assert that I see a cat unless I were seeing a cat, and so forth. Whether pointing to these counterfactuals is providing a sufficient explanation of what it is for the word "cat" to refer to cats is another question. But that question can be discussed whether or not the foregoing evolutionary speculations are true. In fact, as a biologist once remarked to me, people often forget that while biological evolution is Darwinian, cultural evolution is Lamarckian. What he meant, of course, is that in the case of cultural evolution we do see the inheritance of acquired characteristics, and there is no mystery about this. Suppose that, in fact, language is primarily the result of cultural evolution rather than of biological evolution, and that proto-concepts and so on play only a marginal role. The explanation of reference just suggested (using counterfactuals) would be no better and no worse off. If the idea is to give an account of intentionality by using counterfactuals, then we may as well discuss that idea directly, on its own merits, without the long detour through the at-present totally unproved speculations about our evolutionary history.[10]

Of course, that evolutionary theory does not answer Kant's riddle as to how anything in the mind can be a representation of anything outside the mind does not mean that there is anything wrong with evolutionary theory, just as the fact that physics does not answer the riddle of the nature of free will and that brain science does not explain induction and language learning does not mean that there is anything wrong with physics or brain science. But I shall not belabor this point. I hope that these first two chapters have helped us to recall how different philosophical and scientific questions actually are, without denying that philosophy needs to be informed by the best available scientific knowledge. In the next chapter I shall look at an attempt by a well-known philosopher of cognitive science to solve Kant's problem—a philosopher who certainly appreciates that lower-level sciences will not, in and of themselves, solve Kant's problem (the puzzle of the existence of "intentionality", as it has come to be called), but who does think that it is possible to give an account, and who has put forward such an account for our consideration.

3

A Theory of Reference

In the preceding chapters I have tried to show that present-day science does not provide a sketch of an "absolute conception of the world", a sketch of a final metaphysics. In this chapter I will address an attempt by a well-known philosopher of cognitive science to solve Kant's problem, the problem of explaining the referential connection between our "representations" and the world. Jerry Fodor is one of the best-known philosophers of language working out of modern linguistic theory, especially the theories of Noam Chomsky, and he himself has been an important contributor to the field of psycholinguistics. Fodor's philosophy sometimes provokes violent disagreement (I disagree with much of it) but it is always enormously stimulating, and fertile in ideas. The new work is no exception. I find it of interest both intrinsically and also metaphilosophically—that is, from the point of view of what it reveals about contemporary philosophy.

Fodor's new theory[1] is rather complicated. I shall describe it in broad outline. For our purposes, we may consider the theory as beginning just where the discussion ended in the last chapter: Fodor examines an attempt to explain just what reference is using counterfactuals, points out what the problem is—and the problem is very closely related to the problems I discussed in the previous chapter—and then proposes a solution, namely the notion of "asymmetric dependence". I need to introduce Fodor's terminology, however.

Suppose someone makes an assertion which contains a token of the English word "cat". In such a case, we shall say for short that the person has performed an act of " 'cat' tokening". Cats cause "cat" tokenings, but so do many other things; for example, I may see a picture of a cat and utter a sentence containing the word "cat". In addition, I may utter the word "cat" simply because I see the letters C-A-T, or because someone else asks me to repeat the word "cat", but we shall exclude these purely syntactic causes of "cat" tokenings from the discussion by fiat. We shall be interested in cases in which something extralinguistic causes a "cat" tokening.

Let us look a little more at the remark I just made, that is:

(1) Cats cause "cat" tokenings.

Fodor refers to this statement as a "law", but it is important to understand the notion of a law that he has in mind.

Fodor is not thinking of laws in the sense in which Carnap thought of laws, that is, statements of fundamental physics which we can express as differential equations, or anything of that kind.[2] Fodor regards it as highly unrealistic (and of course I agree) to expect that linguistics should model its notion of law on the notion of law employed in fundamental physics. Linguistics, Fodor thinks, should be regarded as one of the "special sciences"[3]—like geology or evolutionary biology—which do not pretend to arrive at *exceptionless* universal generalizations. If geologists say that, other things being equal, rocks belonging to stratum A will always be found below rocks belonging to stratum B, Fodor will call this statement a law even though it contains the phrase "other things being equal". Laws containing these "other things being equal" clauses (Fodor calls them *ceteris paribus* clauses) are still able to support counterfactuals in many

situations, and they enter into explanations which are fundamental in the particular special science, even if they are not
fundamental in the sense that mathematical physics is fundamental. Of course, the statement that cats cause "cat" tokenings
does not even mean that, other things being equal, a cat will
cause a "cat" tokening. It rather means that cats frequently
cause "cat" tokenings, or, perhaps, that they cause "cat" tokenings more often than any one other kind of object causes "cat"
tokenings.[4] But that is all right too, because all of the special
sciences need to make statements about what is frequently the
case, as well as statements about what is always the case, or
what is always the case other things being equal.

Now, the idea that Fodor is trying to work out is that what
a word refers to is a matter of its causal "attachments to the
world".[5] At least in basic cases, what a word W refers to is
going to be a matter of what causes W tokenings. But it is
obvious that not everything that causes a W tokening is referred
to by the word W. We already mentioned that pictures of cats
cause "cat" tokenings, and the word "cat" does not refer to
pictures of cats. Statues of cats and plastic cats may also cause
"cat" tokenings. A meow may cause a "cat" tokening. And so
on. The problem, then, is: given that there are many truths of
the form

(2) Xs cause "cat" tokenings,

how can we determine which of these truths is fundamental,
in the sense that it represents or determines the reference of the
word "cat"?

Note that Fodor's question is not: what does such-and-such
a particular token of the word "cat" refer to? On a particular
occasion, a token of the word "cat" may very well refer to a cat
in a picture, or to a cat statue and not to a cat. Fodor's problem

is to determine the "basic" meaning of the *type* word "cat". (What he wants to say about token reference, I do not know.)

Fodor's answer is that there is a *dependence relation* among truths of the form (2), and that this dependence relation is *asymmetric*. The dependence is expressed by a counterfactual:

(3) If cats didn't cause "cat" tokenings, then the other things that we mentioned (cat pictures, cat statues, the sound "meow", and so on) wouldn't cause "cat" tokenings either.

In Fodor's terminology, the "law"

(4) Pictures of cats cause "cat" tokenings

depends on the "law" that cats cause "cat" tokenings, but not vice versa, and it is this asymmetric dependence that determines the position of the law "cats cause 'cat' tokenings" at the top of the hierarchy of laws of the form (2). The fact that this law is at the top of the hierarchy is what makes it the case that the word "cat" refers to cats and not to pictures of cats, statues of cats, occurrences of the sound "meow", and so forth.

Is the Dependence Really Asymmetric?

The first thing we have to consider is whether the dependence Fodor is talking about really exists and whether it is really asymmetric. The first question reduces to this: is it really true that if cats didn't cause "cat" tokenings, then pictures of cats wouldn't cause "cat" tokenings either?

Fodor's thought is that if cats didn't cause "cat" tokenings then that would most likely be because the word "cat" didn't refer to cats. In the jargon of possible worlds semanticists,[6] the idea is that the "closest possible worlds" (that is the possible worlds which are closest to the actual world) in which cats don't cause "cat" tokenings are possible worlds in which the word "cat" refers to something else altogether. This seems reasonable (at least it seems reasonable if we take "possible worlds" to be hypothetical situations that are relevant to the truth value of a counterfactual, and not real worlds), so let us accept this for the sake of the argument. This shows that the dependence exists—that the "law" "cat pictures cause 'cat' tokenings" *depends on* the law "cats cause 'cat' tokenings"—but it doesn't suffice to show that the dependence is asymmetric. To show that the dependence is asymmetric, we have to show that it is not the case that *if cat pictures didn't cause "cat" tokenings, then cats wouldn't cause "cat" tokenings either.* Fodor takes this to be obvious, but is it?

Wouldn't it be reasonable to suppose that the closest possible worlds in which it isn't a "law" that cat pictures cause "cat" tokenings are possible worlds in which most people have no idea what cats look like? If we take those to be the closest possible worlds in which cat pictures don't cause "cat" tokenings, then it would be the case that if cat pictures didn't cause "cat" tokenings, then cats wouldn't cause "cat" tokenings either, and the dependence would be *symmetric*.

One possible counter would be for Fodor simply to insist on the "intuition" that among those possible worlds in which cat pictures do not cause "cat" tokenings, the closest ones are the ones in which people are blind, or can't recognize things in pictures, or otherwise have a nature which is very different from actual human nature, and not the ones in which people don't know what cats look like. But this seems implausible.

A better move, I think, would be for Fodor to say that by "cats cause 'cat' tokenings" he means not that cats frequently cause "cat" tokenings, but that they sometimes cause "cat" tokenings. To this one might object that this claim is too weak; after all, isn't it the case that

(5) For every observable kind of thing X, and for every word W, Xs sometimes cause W tokenings?

One can think of some far-fetched situation, for example, in which the sight of an apple will cause me to mention dogs,[7] or the sight of a pig will cause me to mention the moon. I think I know what Fodor would say about such cases. I think he would say that while it may be true that

(6) Apples sometimes cause "cat" tokenings,

that truth is not "lawlike". ("Lawlikeness" is a primitive notion in Fodor's metaphysics; moreover, it is a relation between universals and not a property of sentences, according to Fodor, which is how he meets the objection that using the notion of lawlikeness is employing a notion which is itself intentional.) While I have doubts about the supposedly non-intentional character of this notion, I shall, for the sake of argument, concede it to Fodor.

Now, even if ordinary people had no idea what cats look like, if the word "cat" continued to refer to cats, there would presumably be at least some people (biologists and other specialists) who still knew what cats looked like. And therefore there would still be some cases in which cats still caused "cat" tokenings (unless we imagine a case in which the species has become extinct, which would perhaps raise still further problems for Fodor's theory). If the closest possible worlds in which ordinary people do not know what cats look like are still possible worlds in which some people do know what cats look like, then in those possible worlds it is still true that *cats sometimes cause "cat" tokenings*, and hence the existence of those "possible worlds" and their "closeness to the actual world" does not establish that the counterfactual *if cat pictures didn't (sometimes) cause "cat" tokenings, then cats wouldn't (sometimes) cause "cat" tokenings* is true. It is still possible for Fodor to maintain that the dependence relation between the "laws" "cats cause 'cat' tokenings" and "pictures of cats cause 'cat' tokenings" is asymmetric. But even if we assume, for the sake of argument, that Fodor's claims are correct, at least in the case of ordinary natural kind words like "cat", it does not necessarily follow that the theory does succeed in providing necessary and sufficient conditions for reference.

In fact, the theory fails badly when the word in question is one whose extension is determined by an analytic necessary and sufficient definition. For example, let us suppose that someone introduces a word for someone whose wealth is at least a hundred billion dollars, say, "superbillionaire". Let us imagine that there are a small number, perhaps five or six, superbillionaires in the world, but that these people either have not heard of this neologism or despise it so much that they and their friends and families and close coworkers and bankers do not use it. Suppose that the half-dozen superbillionaires successfully conceal the fact that they are superbillionaires from the general public; the general public knows that they are billionaires but has no idea that they are superbillionaires. Then it could be that there is no single case in which a superbillionaire ever causes a "superbillionaire" tokening; yet it would still be true that "superbillionaire" refers to superbillionaires. Again there are a number of possible responses Fodor might make. He might, for example, say that *if people knew all the relevant facts*, then superbillionaires would cause "superbillionaire" tokenings. But what is a relevant fact depends on the *meaning* of the word we are considering. To know, that is, what the reference of "superbillionaire" is, using the criterion that "if people knew all the relevant facts, then superbillionaires would cause 'superbillionaire' tokenings", we would have to know what facts are relevant to determining the truth value of such sentences as "X is a superbillionaire", and this would require having *already* interpreted "superbillionaire".

Fodor might say that if English speakers were omniscient,

then superbillionaires would cause "superbillionaire" tokenings. But omniscience is not only a non-actual state of affairs but an impossible state of affairs for human beings. Alternatively—and this is, I think, the most plausible line for Fodor to take—Fodor might say that his theory is not meant to apply to words which have analytic definitions.[8] The trouble with this reply is that the whole raison d'être of Fodor's theory is to be anti-hermeneutic; that is, Fodor rejects the view that one cannot determine the reference of a word in a language in isolation. According to hermeneuticists, whether of the Gadamerian variety or of the Davidsonian variety, to interpret a language one must make tentative assignments of extensions, that is, of reference, to the words; proceed to see whether the speakers of the language come out talking sense or nonsense according to these reference assignments; and then make adjustments in the tentative reference assignments until one finally ends up with an interpretation which makes maximum sense of the linguistic behavior of the people being interpreted. According to hermeneuticists there can be no such thing as necessary and sufficient conditions for a word W to refer to Xs. The best we can hope for are criteria of adequacy for translation schemes, or reference assignments, or assignments of truth-conditions. This view, the hermeneutic view, is anathema to Fodor. It leads, according to him, to "meaning holism", which in turn leads to "meaning nihilism",[9] which leads to the denial of the possibility of a "special science" of linguistics. To determine whether a word in a language has an analytic definition or not, what we need is precisely an *interpretation* of the language. If Fodor's theory of reference applies only to a class of words, not to all the words of the language, and we can determine whether a word belongs to the class to which it applies only by first interpreting the language, then the theory does not do what Fodor wants it to do. It does not provide us with a reductive and non-holistic account of reference in terms of "causal attachment".

Fodor might reply that the theory is really meant to apply not to natural language but to his hypothetical innate language of thought, "Mentalese".[10] According to Fodor, all the concepts that appear in all natural languages are already available in Mentalese, available *innately*, and Fodor may well think that the innate structure of Mentalese determines which concepts have, and which do not have, analytic definitions. But if this is his view, then his entire theory is of no interest to those of us who find the idea that all concepts are innate preposterous.

In any case, Fodor's theory fails on still other kinds of words as well. Consider the word "witch".[11] It may be analytic that true witches have magical powers and that they are female; but having magical powers and being female is not a necessary and sufficient condition for being a witch. Many female saints are ascribed magical powers, but they are not considered witches. Nor must a witch have magical powers which come from an evil source or which are used for evil; anyone who has read *The Wizard of Oz* knows that there are good witches as well as evil witches. The word "witch" seems to have expanded its semantic range through a process of "family resemblance". The first witches to be mentioned in the Bible are, in fact, pagan witches; the characteristic Christian witch who has sold her soul to the Devil represents a much later idea. The problem posed by the word "witch" is that the "law"

(6) Witches cause "witch" tokenings,

is false. There are no witches to cause "witch" tokenings.

I believe that Fodor would meet this objection by saying that still it is counterfactually true that

(7) If there were witches, they would cause "witch" token-ings.

But it is far from clear that this is true. If a witch must have magical powers, then it is far from clear that the concept of a witch is a coherent one, because it is far from clear that the concept of a magical power is a coherent one. We can certainly imagine possible worlds in which things regularly happen that superstitious people would regard as magic; but the very fact that they regularly happen in those possible worlds is strong reason for saying that in those possible worlds those things are not really magic—it is just that those worlds have different laws than the actual world. The notion of a world in which things happen that are "truly magical" is, I think, an incoherent one; and that means, I think, that the notion of a witch is an incoherent one.

One might try to meet this difficulty by defining a witch not as someone who has magical powers but as someone who has supernatural powers, where the supernatural is understood not in terms of the notion of magic, but in terms of not falling within the categories of substance, space, and time. It is extremely doubtful that the pagan witches, or the witches of present-day African tribes, are supposed to derive their powers from something which is supernatural in that sense. It is a feature, in fact, of pagan thought that the gods, demons, and so on, are not supernatural in the sense which came into existence with the rise of Greek philosophy and the incorporation into the Jerusalem-based religions of a certain amount of Greek philosophy. The notion that what is magical must derive from the supernatural, in the philosophical/theological sense of "supernatural", is not part of the original meaning of the term.

If the existence of witches is incoherent, then there are no possible worlds in which there are witches, and then (7) is senseless. But let us be charitable and suppose that somehow coherent sense can be made of the notion of a witch, and that there are possible worlds in which there are witches. Then, Fodor might say, the counterfactual (7), "if there were witches, they would cause 'witch' tokenings", is true. This, he might claim, is the "law" at the top of the relevant hierarchy generated by the asymmetric dependence relation.

If this counterfactual is true—and I have just given reasons for thinking it isn't—then its truth is certainly not explained by natural law. For this counterfactual refers to what would be the case if some beings really had magical powers. If it is a truth that "in the closest possible worlds in which there are beings of a certain kind with magical powers, those beings cause 'witch' tokenings among English speakers", then that truth is certainly not a truth which belongs to any natural science. It would, in fact, be a metaphysical truth. If Fodor's theory succeeded in this case, it would not provide a reduction of reference to the notions of the special sciences considered as natural sciences, but a reduction of the notion of reference to some very suspicious metaphysical notions. Similarly, if Fodor has to appeal to counterfactuals about what people would say if they were omniscient, he will again have to appeal to counterfactuals whose antecedent is physically impossible—impossible on the basis of natural law—and this involves the same kind of metaphysics.

Now let us consider a perfectly ordinary word, "soldier". It is perfectly true that

(8) Soldiers cause "soldier" tokenings.

But it is also true that

(9) People who pretend to be soldiers cause "soldier" token-ings.

For the right "asymmetric dependence" to hold between these two "laws", it is necessary that the following counterfactual be false:

(10) If people who pretend to be soldiers didn't cause "soldier" tokenings, then soldiers wouldn't cause "soldier" to-kenings.

Now, of course, there is something funny about all of the counterfactuals that Fodor needs. For example, the counterfac-tual "if cats didn't cause 'cat' tokenings, then pictures of cats wouldn't cause 'cat' tokenings either" is not one that would ever be heard in ordinary life. If someone asked me "What would happen if cats didn't cause 'cat' tokenings?" my response would be to ask "What situation do you have in mind?". If the person said, "well, suppose the word 'cat' referred to a different kind of thing", then I might know how to evaluate various counter-factuals about what would happen if cats didn't cause "cat" tokenings. But to say that what I am to imagine is that the word "cat" has a different reference would be to beg the whole ques-tion, for Fodor's whole enterprise is to define reference without appeal to any notions which presuppose it. To do this, he must assume that counterfactuals like "if cats didn't cause 'cat' token-ings, then pictures of cats wouldn't cause 'cat' tokenings *either*" already have a truth value—that the semantics of counterfac-tuals (whatever that may come to) already assigns a truth value to such bizarre counterfactuals. If we are going to play that game, however, then I don't see why we shouldn't say that if people who pretend to be soldiers didn't cause "soldier" token-ings, that would almost certainly be because the word "soldier" had a different reference. After all, wouldn't we expect that as long as the word "soldier" continues to mean soldier, then people who tell other people that they are soldiers cause "soldier" tokenings?

If the closest possible worlds in which people who pretend to be soldiers do not cause "soldier" tokenings are the worlds in which "soldier" has a different reference, however, then the counterfactual "if people who pretend to be soldiers didn't cause 'soldier' tokenings, then soldiers wouldn't cause 'soldier' tokenings" is true, and not false as the asymmetric dependence theory requires.

Fodor would perhaps say that if people were able to distinguish pretend soldiers from real soldiers infallibly, then soldiers would cause "soldier" tokenings, but people pretending to be soldiers would not cause "soldier" tokenings; but worlds in which people have such extraordinary abilities would seem to be extremely far from the actual world. Moreover, the notion of knowledge which is involved in the description of such possible worlds is itself one which presupposes the possession of a language, that is, the ability to *refer*.

Fodor's Notion of a Cause

In this discussion I have not questioned Fodor's free use of the notion of something causing something else, e.g., a cat causing an event which is a "cat" tokening. But let us examine this notion a little more closely. The notion of cause in ordinary language is both context bound and interest dependent, as Hart and Honoré pointed out many years ago.[12] For example, if John eats foods high in cholesterol for many years and refuses to exercise, against the advice of his doctor and even though he has been told he has high blood pressure, and as a result suffers a heart attack, we may say that (i) his failure to exercise and eat a proper diet caused the heart attack, or that (ii) his high

blood pressure caused the heart attack, depend_ng on the context and our interests. If fact, even if A is a contributory cause
of B we are unlikely to refer to A as "a cause" of B unless A is
the sort of contributory cause that it would be natural to refer
to as "the cause" of B in at least some contexts. For example,
if a pressure cooker has a stuck valve and explodes, the absence
of holes in the vessel of the pressure cooker is clearly a contributory cause of the explosion, as any engineer will tell you,
but we would never in ordinary language say that the absence
of holes in the vessel of the pressure cooker was "the cause" of
the explosion, nor would we normally say

(11) The absence of holes in the vessel of the pressure cooker
was a cause of the explosion,

although we would say that the stuck valve caused the explosion
(and to say that a valve is stuck just means that there isn't a
hole in a certain place where there ought to be a hole).

The notion of cause that Fodor is using is just this ordinary-
language, context-sensitive, interest-relative notion, and not
the relatively more context-independent notion of contributory
cause.

To see this, consider what would happen if we tried to
interpret Fodor's theory using the notion of contributory cause
as the relevant notion. When Fodor says "cats cause 'cat' tokenings", what he means on this interpretation is that the
presence of a cat is a contributory cause of many cat tokenings.
But then it is certainly true that the past behavior of English
speakers (not to mention speakers of Anglo-Saxon and other
ancestors of English) is also a contributory cause of "cat" tokenings, since we would not be using the word at all if the past
linguistic behavior of English speakers (Anglo-Saxon speakers,
etc.) had been different. So

(12) The past behavior of English speakers causes "cat" tokenings

would also be true on this interpretation of causes; that is, the
past linguistic behavior of English speakers is a contributory
cause of "cat" tokenings. What is the relation of counterfactual
dependence between (12) and "cats cause 'cat' tokenings"? Is
the dependence asymmetrical? And if so, in which direction is
the asymmetry?

Well, if cats didn't cause "cat" tokenings, the word "cat"
would probably mean something else (this assumption is essential to Fodor's whole argument), but even if it meant something
else, as long as it was still a word in English, it would still be
the case that the past behavior of English speakers was a contributory cause of present "cat" tokenings. It is not true that

(13) If cats didn't cause "cat" tokenings, then the past behavior
of English speakers wouldn't cause (be a contributory cause of)
"cat" tokenings.

On the other hand, if the past behavior of English speakers
were not a contributory cause of "cat" tokenings, that would
almost certainly have to be because "cat" wasn't a word in the
language. Thus it is reasonable to say that the set of closest
possible worlds in which the past behavior of English speakers
is not a contributory cause of "cat" tokenings is the set of possible
worlds in which the word "cat" is not a word in the English
language. If so, then the following counterfactual is true:

(14) If the past behavior of English speakers didn't cause
(wasn't a contributory cause of) "cat" tokenings, then cats
wouldn't cause "cat" tokenings.

On this interpretation of "cause" as "contributory cause", (i)
the dependence *is* asymmetrical, and (ii) the dependence goes
the wrong way for Fodor's theory.

However, this is, as I said, pretty clearly *not* the interpretation of cause that Fodor has in mind. All of his examples, as well as his references to other special sciences like geology, indicate that he simply wishes to take the ordinary-language notion of cause as primitive. What is strange about this, is that this notion of causation is interest relative. Whether we say that A caused B or not depends on what we take to be the relevant alternatives. If we are interested in what would have happened to John if he had obeyed the doctor's orders, then we are likely to say that his eating habits and lack of exercise caused his heart attack, but if we are interested in what would have happened to John if he had not had high blood pressure to begin with, then we are likely to say that his high blood pressure caused the heart attack. Notice that being interested in something involves, albeit in a slightly hidden way, the notion of "aboutness", that is, the central intentional notion. To be interested in something, in this sense, you have to be able to think about it—you have to be able to refer to it, in thought or in language. Fodor uses a notion which has an intentional dimension; his notion of things "causing" other things is not a notion which is simply handed to us by physics. For in fundamental physics at least, one usually ignores the distinction between contributory causes and "the cause", and tries to provide a formalism which shows how all of the factors interact to produce the final result.

Moreover, Fodor assumes that counterfactuals have definite truth values, including many counterfactuals that would baffle any ordinary speaker. Here his defense is that counterfactuals are used in geology, evolutionary biology, and other "special sciences". He might also say that I have made his use of counterfactuals look more suspect than it is by referring to the possible-worlds semantics for counterfactuals. Perhaps Fodor would reject the possible-worlds semantics. He could certainly say that, whatever the status of that semantics, all he is assuming is that counterfactuals make sense and have truth values, not that it makes sense to talk about possible worlds, or about possible worlds being closer to or farther away from the actual world. This would certainly be fair; and I did not mean, in using this vocabulary, to indicate that I myself regard possible-worlds talk as metaphysically satisfactory, or that I regard talk of closeness of possible worlds as *explaining* how it is that counterfactuals are true. The possible-worlds semantics, as I see it, is simply a model which enables us to formalize the deductive relations among counterfactuals, and no more. But that formalism does have a close connection with counterfactuals in the following way: just looking at how we employ counterfactuals, we will notice that—even if we think of possible worlds as mere stories or hypothetical situations—we do not treat all possible worlds in which the antecedent is true as equally relevant to the truth of a counterfactual. If I say "If I had put this lump of sugar in my coffee, it would have dissolved", then there are an enormous number of possible worlds in which the antecedent of that counterfactual is true—that is, there are an enormous number of hypothetical situations in which the antecedent is true—but I do not regard all of them as relevant. In the case of that counterfactual, for example, I would ignore hypothetical situations in which the laws of physics are different. From some counterfactuals that exclusion, of hypothetical situations in which the laws of physics are not as they are in the actual world, suffices. If A and B are related in such a way that the material conditional "if A, then B" follows deductively from a finite set of true laws of physics, then the counterfactual "if A were the case, then B would be the case" is certainly true. For counterfactuals of this kind—I have elsewhere called them "strict counterfactuals"—a "similarity metric on possible worlds" is easy to specify: a world is "sufficiently close" to the actual world just in case it obeys the same laws of physics as are true in the actual world. But many counterfactuals are considered as true even though there exists some physically possible world in which the antecedent is true and the consequent is false. For example, there are physically possible worlds in which a lump of sugar is put in hot coffee and does not dissolve. This is true because of entropy considerations and also because of quantum mechanical considerations.[13] We regard these possible worlds as somehow too abnormal to falsify the counterfactual "if I had put the sugar in the coffee it would have dissolved". So even if we drop the language of "possible worlds", and drop the language of possible words being "closer to" or "farther away from" the actual world, we still have to recognize that a counterfactual may be true even though there exists a hypothetical situation (one representable as a physical state of affairs in the formalism of physics) in which the antecedent of the counterfactual is true, all the fundamental physical laws which hold in the actual world hold in the hypothetical situation, and the consequent of the counterfactual is false. Indeed, almost all of the counterfactuals that we use in the special sciences are of this kind. For this reason, we may say that the very use of counterfactuals, whether it explicitly presupposes a similarity metric on possible worlds or not, implicitly determines such a metric. By looking at which counterfactuals we count as true, we can see which hypothetical situations we consider more relevant to determining the truth value of the counterfactual and which we consider irrelevant (or abnormal); and if we call the more relevant ones "closer", then it does not seem that any great harm will be done.

Still, Fodor might reply, this way of looking at the situation is misleading because it gives an unreasonable pride of place to the laws of physics, that is, it gives too much weight to what is physically possible and what is physically impossible, and not enough weight to "laws" in another sense, the laws of the special sciences. Why should we, after all, emphasize possible worlds which can be represented as states of affairs in the physicist's sense—regions in phase space, states of affairs whose time-development obeys the laws of fundamental physics, possible worlds in which nothing "physically impossible" happens? If we think of such states of affairs as unproblematic, and then think inherently problematic any selection from those states of affairs which involves treating some of them as more relevant than others, then, of course, we will be led to look for something like a "similarity metric on possible worlds" in order to account for the fact that there are true counterfactuals which are not what I called "strict counterfactuals". (Another motive for looking at possible-worlds semantics, a very different one, is to have some account of the truth of some counterfactuals whose antecedents are physically impossible.)

To meet this objection, suppose we took the view that the laws of the special sciences are *just* as unproblematic as the laws of physics, and that it is at least a sufficient condition for the truth of a counterfactual that (i) there are situations in which the antecedent holds and in which *all laws of nature* (not just the laws of fundamental physics) hold; and (ii) the consequent holds in all those states of affairs. This suggestion doesn't quite work (which may be why Fodor does not put it forward).

To see that it does not work, consider again the counterfactual "if I had put this lump of sugar in my coffee, it would have dissolved". According to the suggestion being considered, that counterfactual is true if the lump of sugar dissolves in all hypothetical situations in which it is put into the coffee and all the laws of the special sciences, including laws with an "other things being equal" clause in them, hold. Now, the suggestion may seem to work, because one law of ordinary chemistry— which is certainly a "special science"—is "other things being equal, a piece of sugar will dissolve in hot coffee". But things are not so simple. For the truth of the statement that other things being equal a piece of sugar will dissolve if put into hot coffee is perfectly compatible with its being the case that *this* piece of sugar will not dissolve if put into hot coffee. It could be the case that *this* piece of sugar is in some way "not normal". The truth of a law of the form "other things being equal, an A will do B in circumstances C" does not imply that any *particular* A will do B in circumstances C, nor does it imply any counterfactual of the form "this particular A would have done B if it had been in circumstances C". This is why I think that Fodor doesn't want one to try to give necessary and sufficient conditions for the truth of a counterfactual using any notion of "law", not even his broadened notion.

Here is what I myself think about counterfactuals: I think that what makes a counterfactual true is simply that the consequent follows from the antecedent together with various relevant natural laws or general truths, plus the initial and boundary conditions in those situations that it would be reasonable to regard as compatible with the intentions of the speaker who uttered the counterfactual. By this I don't mean to suppose that a speaker who utters a counterfactual can *imagine* all conditions that might be relevant to what the speaker has in mind. To describe the conditions which are relevant to what he or she has in mind might require quantum mechanics, for example, or even some physical theory which has not yet been thought of, or some theory in some other science which has not yet been thought of. What I am saying is that an evaluator of the counterfactual who does know the relevant theories, and who thinks of some case in which the antecedent of the counterfactual is true and the consequent of the counterfactual is false, must decide whether the case actually falsifies the counterfactual, or whether it is more reasonable to think that the case is too far-fetched to be relevant to what the speaker intended to say. In effect, the evaluator imagines himself as being the speaker, and as having the same intentions as the original speaker, but with much more knowledge of natural science, or whatever, than the original speaker. Fodor would presumably reject this suggestion because it implies that counterfactuals ineliminably presuppose the point of view of reason. To say that taking into account one state of affairs is "reasonable" while taking another state of affairs into account would be "unreasonable" is to make a normative judgment; and what I am going to argue in the lectures to come is that the desire to leave all normative considerations out of the philosophy of language is precisely what leads to the failure of the various attempts to "naturalize the intentional".

Fodor's Metaphysical Picture

Let me now say a word or two about Fodor's metaphilosophical stance. It is clear that Fodor's aim is to provide a reductive account of reference in the following sense: he views the special sciences which do not especially refer to the human race, sciences like evolutionary biology and geology, as somehow belonging to the realm of the non-intentional (or the pre-intentional).[14] These sciences describe reality as it is, in itself, before symbol users and referers appear on the scene. Moreover, he seems to think[15] that any concept which is essential to such a special science is philosophically kosher, that is, is a concept which we have a philosophical right to regard as unproblematic.[16] (This is somewhat strange, since one would think offhand that what we have a right to regard as unproblematic should depend on the question being asked.) Geology uses laws with "other things being equal" clauses in them; therefore, "other things being equal" is an unproblematic notion which we can use anywhere in philosophy. Geology uses the ordinary notion of something causing something else; therefore the ordinary notion of causation is an unproblematic notion which we can use anywhere in philosophy. Geology uses counterfactual conditionals, therefore the counterfactual conditional is an unproblematic notion which we can use anywhere in philosophy.

I certainly agree that there is nothing wrong with a geologist, or an evolutionary biologist, or a psychologist, or whoever, using a counterfactual conditional, or saying that something is the cause of something else, for that matter. My opposition to Fodor is by no means diametrical. Fodor's view has both a reductionist and an anti-reductionist element. Fodor is anti-reductionist in that he does not think that the special sciences can be reduced to fundamental physics. He has argued for many years and very persuasively that it is impossible to require geology or evolutionary biology or psychology to use only concepts which are definable in terms of the concepts we need to do mathematical physics. This anti-reductionist side of Fodor's thought is one that I hail. Fodor also recognizes that the nature of reference and the nature of general intelligence are not questions to which present-day Artificial Intelligence offers even a sketch of an answer. He would have no quarrel, as far as I can see, with the arguments I advanced in the first chapter. At the same time, however, Fodor clings to the picture of the natural sciences—that is, the sciences below psychology—as describing the world as it is independent of intentional or cognitive notions, a ready-made world. His anti-reductionism simply leads him to view any notion used by those sciences as descriptive of what is "out there" independent of mind and independent of language users. If geology needs counterfactual conditionals, then counterfactual conditionals are "out there"; if geology needs to say that something causes something else, then causation (in that sense) is "out there". His retention of the old desire to reduce consciousness and mind to something wholly physical remains, but in an altered form, as the desire to reduce the central intentional notion, the notion of reference, to these notions. It is this reductionist side of Fodor's thought that I reject. But I have argued here that even if I give Fodor all that he wants to use—his notion of "law", his peculiar counterfactual conditionals, his notion of causation—still he has not successfully defined reference in such terms. The reduction has failed.

On Fodor's picture, just as physicists discovered at a certain stage of the game that you cannot give a complete description of the world in terms of the forces known to classical physics alone, and so had to add new primitives in order to talk about new forces—for example the so-called "strong force" that holds the nucleus of the atom together—so geologists and biologists discovered that, just as the strong force and the weak force and mass and charge are out there in the world, independent of mind, so "ceteris-paribus-hood" (or "other-things-being-equal-ness") is out there in the world, independent of mind, and one thing's "causing" another is out there in the world, independent of mind, and something's being a "law" is out there in the world, independent of mind. It is at this point that Fodor and I part company. From the fact that a statement is not explicitly about anything mental it does not follow that none of its presuppositions make any reference to our cognitive interests, our way of regarding different contexts, or our intentional powers. I have argued that the notion of causation, for example, has a cognitive dimension, even when we use it in a statement about inanimate objects, for example the statement that the stuck valve caused the pressure cooker to explode. The cognitive or "intentional" dimension lies in part in the presupposition that hearers of the statement regard such facts as that the vessel of the pressure cooker does not have a hole in it as "background conditions" which may be taken for granted, as well as in our knowledge of the salience that others attach to the condition of the valve. When I say that the water would have boiled if the gas stove had been turned on, there is an even more complex cognitive dimension.

If Fodor (the side of Fodor that I agree with) is right, and ordinary-language notions of causation (as opposed to the technical notions used in mathematical physics), and ordinary-language counterfactual conditionals, and ordinary-language notions of scientific law (however much Fodor may overblow and distort both counterfactual conditionals and the ordinary notion of scientific law) are essential in sciences which do not deal especially with human beings (like geology or evolutionary biology), what that shows is not that the statement that one thing caused another has no intentional dimension, but rather that concepts which do have an intentional dimension, concepts whose very use presupposes an identification with the interests and saliencies of human beings rather than a "view from nowhere", are indispensable even when we talk about rocks or species.

To deny, as I do, that there is a "ready-made world" is not to say that we make up the world. I am not denying that there are geological facts which we did not make up. But I have long argued that to ask which facts are mind independent in the sense that nothing about them reflects our conceptual choices and which facts are "contributed by us" is to commit a "fallacy of division". What we say about the world reflects our conceptual choices and our interests, but its truth or falsity is not simply determined by our conceptual choices and our interests. To try to divide the world into a part that is independent of us and a part that is contributed by us is an old temptation, but giving in to it leads to disaster every time. If one accepts this point of view, then both the successes of Fodor's criticism of reductionism with respect to the special sciences and the failures of his own attempt at reductionism with respect to semantics take on a different aspect. It does not look as if the intentional can simply be reduced to the non-intentional; rather, it begins to look as if the intentional intrudes even into our description of the non-intentional, as if the intentional (or, better, the cognitive) is to some extent ubiquitous.

One thing that interests me in this book is why we are so reluctant to admit this. What does it show about our culture and our entire way of thinking that it is so hard for us to admit this, and what might a philosophy might be like that began to give up all reductionist dreams?

4

Materialism and Relativism

While individual philosophers continue to produce and defend as wide a range of metaphysical views as they ever have, today two outlooks have become dominant in American and French philosophy; these are, respectively, the outlooks of materialism and of relativism. Although few American philosophers actually call themselves materialists, and I do not know of any French philosophers who actually call themselves relativists, the terms "physicalism" and "naturalism" have become virtually synonymous with materialism in analytic philosophy, while the thrust of deconstructionist views is often clearly relativist, if not downright nihilist. I have argued for some years that both styles of thought are too simplistic to be much help in philosophical reflection.[1]

I have already indicated some reasons for my dissatisfaction with materialism as an ideology. The materialist philosopher believes that present-day scientific theories already contain the broad outlines of a solution to philosophical problems about the nature of minds and intentionality; I have argued that there is no reason to believe that this is the case. However, my purpose here is not to polemicize against materialism and relativism, but to see what we can learn from the failure of these large points of view. There are, happily, many philosophers who reject both relativism and semantic materialism, that is, reject the idea that the semantical is going to be reduced to the physical, or even to the concepts of the "special sciences" which do not explicitly use intentional notions; but I often sense the feeling, especially among students, that the abandonment of these totalistic programs may mean the "end of philosophy". Indeed, Richard Rorty[2] has very strongly defended the view that philosophy is, in a certain sense, at an end and we must ready ourselves for a post-philosophical era. I don't think this is at all the right moral to draw from the present situation, but before we can see what the right moral is, we need to ask in more detail just where materialism and relativism have gone wrong.

Chomskian Fears of "Interest Relativity"

I begin by contrasting Jerry Fodor's attitude toward the concepts he takes as primitive—causation and the counterfactual conditional—and my own attitude as I sketched it in the last chapter. In my opinion, counterfactual conditionals and causal statements presuppose what I call "the point of view of reason".

What I mean by this is that, for example, when we evaluate a counterfactual conditional (unless the counterfactual conditional is what I called a "strict" counterfactual conditional)[3] we do not consider all of the physically possible situations in which the antecedent is true; typically, we are aware that there are physically possible situations in which the antecedent is true and the consequent is false, and yet very often we accept the counterfactual conditional as true notwithstanding. If my wife and I sit down to have breakfast, and we discover that I forgot to turn the gas stove on, and so there is no hot water for coffee, my wife might well say, "if you hadn't been so absentminded, and had turned on the stove, we would have hot water for coffee now". I can think of a number of bizarre physical possibilities such that if any one of them had obtained, then I could have turned on the gas stove and yet the water would not have gotten hot. But mentioning any of these possibilities to my wife at that moment is not going to be a very successful strategy. As far as Ruth Anna is concerned—and she is using the counterfactual conditional in a perfectly correct way—her counterfactual is true. And what justifies her in calling it true is her knowledge of the regularity connecting the lighting of the gas stove and the boiling of the water that is put on it, and her knowledge that that regularity fully justifies her expecting that the water will be hot, conditional on my having turned on the gas stove. Note that the bizarre physical possibilities I might think of do not falsify her counterfactual.

That is not to say that Ruth Anna's counterfactual conditional is not defeasible. If it turns out that there was an interruption of the gas pressure in the line, unknown to both of us, and that the gas stove would not have stayed lit even if I had turned it on, then her counterfactual conditional is defeated. Someone might propose that what rules out the bizarre physical situations I mentioned from being relevant is that they are improbable. But if I *had* turned on the gas stove, then the resulting situation would have been different from the actual situation in countless ways (various molecules would have been in different places than they actually were, whole chains of causality would have been set into motion that were not set into motion in the actual world, and so on), and that situation would have certainly had a host of improbable features, since every actual physical situation always has features which are highly improbable. It is not probability as such, but *probability in relevant respects* that counts, and this again brings in what I called the point of view of reason.

To make what is involved clearer, let us suppose that the

person who utters the counterfactual is not Ruth Anna but someone who knows no physics, and that I who hear the counterfactual know a great deal of physics. Even in such a case, I do not count as automatically falsifying the statement the fact that I know of physical situations that the speaker cannot even imagine in which I would have turned on the gas stove and the water would not have boiled. Rather I engage in the following kind of thinking: on the one hand, I put myself in the speaker's shoes, and imagine myself uttering the same counterfactual in the same situation and with the same practical point. At the same time, in evaluating the counterfactual that was uttered (and that I imagine myself as having uttered, in my imaginative identification with the speaker), if I consider it relevant, I take into account my own scientific knowledge, as well as the speaker's reasons and intentions in uttering the counterfactual. I try to decide—of course, in many cases, the decision is quite automatic, or the question does not even arise—whether there are any possible situations that I can think of that *really* falsify the speaker's counterfactual. In particular, if possible situations come to mind in which the antecedent of the counterfactual would be true and the consequent false, then I try to decide whether those situations—situations that falsify the counterfactual if they are relevant—do or do not have that kind of relevance. Possible-worlds semanticists would express this by saying that I try to decide if certain possible worlds are closer to the actual world than certain others.

If there is a criticism to be made of the language used by possible-worlds semanticists, the language of worlds being "closer" or "farther" away from the actual world, it is that that language conceals what needs to be brought out, that what is actually being judged is not the distance of objects from one another in a hyper-space but the relevance of hypothetical situations, and the relevance of situations to a judgment is an essentially normative matter. What using the language of "closeness" does is to make a normative judgment, a judgment as to whether it is *reasonable* to regard something as relevant, sound like a description of a "value-neutral fact".

I have explained my views about counterfactuals and also my views about causation in several publications.[4] Yet a wellknown philosopher asked me recently if I am a "causal nihilist". What is going on here?

It seems to me that this is what happens: when I say that the truth of a judgment of the form A *caused* B depends upon the context and the interests of the people making the judgment (for example, what the speakers want to know in a particular context),[5] then there are those who immediately leap to the conclusion that I must be saying that such judgments are entirely subjective, or, perhaps, that they are entirely arbitrary. This is not simply conjecture on my part. Noam Chomsky reacted in the following way to precisely my claim of the interest-relativity of statements of the form A *explains* B: "Therefore [Putnam] is offering as a substantive metaphysical thesis that correctness in linguistics (and psychology) *is* what best explains the currently available data about the behavior of the speaker given some current interests; what is correct today will be false tomorrow, and what is correct depends on our current interests and purposes."[6] Now, that what is correct today will be false tomorrow is no part of anything I have ever maintained; yet to Chomsky it seems obviously to follow from views like the ones I defended in the previous chapter.

If I am not very much mistaken, Chomsky's main hidden premises are two: (1) that we are free to choose our interests at will; and (2) that interests are not themselves subject to normative criticism. Or perhaps the premise is that what is normative is itself arbitrary and subjective? (This does not seem likely to me in the case of Chomsky, although it is, I think, behind the thinking of some of my other critics.)

Consider the medical example that I used earlier. In one context I may say that John's heart attack was caused by his failure to obey his doctor's orders; he insisted on eating high-cholesterol foods and he refused to exercise. Yet in a different context I may say that John's heart attack was caused by high blood pressure. Assuming that both the high blood pressure and the failure to obey the doctor's orders were important contributory causes, and that I was aware of this in both situations, I certainly would not regard my statement in the second context as contradicting my statement in the first context. If someone said to me "but yesterday you said the cause was his failure to obey doctor's orders", I might well reply "yes, but then the question was what John could have done to avoid the heart attack, and today the question is what physiologically predisposed him to the heart attack". A *caused B* and A' *caused B* may sound incompatible, but they are not, in such a case.

I want to repeat again the two points that seem to me important: (1) We cannot simply choose what interests we have. The language we speak reflects who and what we are, and in particular reflects the kind of interests we have. Since we know the kinds of interests that people do have, we are able to hear what sound like contradictory statements and to understand them in a way which is not contradictory. In case of confusion, we can easily reword these statements in other ways; for instance, we can say "even given his high blood pressure, John would not have had the heart attack if he had obeyed his doctor's orders" and "even given his bad diet and lack of exercise, John would not have had the heart attack if he hadn't had high blood pressure". (2) It does sometimes happen that it is debatable whether a given interest is or is not relevant. If a Marxist says that the cause of John's heart attack was the capitalist system, we are likely to scoff—unless, of course, the Marxist makes a case that wins us over. Whether an interest is or is not relevant is something that can itself be argued. To say that a notion is interest relative is not to say that all interests are equally reasonable.

But what makes some interests more reasonable than others? The answer is that reasonableness depends on different things in different contexts. There is no general answer. The real dividing line here is between philosophers who, either consciously or unconsciously, assume that normative notions are subjective, and hence anything tainted by them must also be subjective, and philosophers who do not start with that assumption. Make the assumption that *normative notions are non-cognitive*; then, of course, any account of explanation, causation, and of the counterfactual conditional which involves normative elements will be heard as making all of these forms of discourse non-cognitive.

Fodor agrees with me that these forms of discourse have cognitive value, but for very different reasons. Fodor responds to those who would deny our right to use counterfactuals and *ceteris paribus* clauses by saying that, after all, we use them in geology (and other "special sciences").[7] Now, what is the significance of the fact that we use them in geology as opposed to the fact that we use them every day of our lives, in the kitchen, as it were? The answer is obvious: geology is a "science". And genuine sciences, Fodor assumes, tell us what we have to assume to be there mind independently. Yet sciences like geology do not pretend to confine themselves to the "primary qualities" of realist metaphysics. Texts in biology are good examples of how we use language in certain kinds of explanations; they are not, and do not pretend to be, an inventory of "the furniture of the universe", and only a bad case of scientism makes a philosopher mistake them for such an inventory.

Relativism

Richard Rorty has been in recent years one of the most important interpreters of continental philosophy to an American audience. Like the continental philosophers that he interprets, Rorty rejects the label "relativist". But almost all of his readers have classified him as some sort of a relativist, and it is not hard to see why, particularly in his *Philosophy and the Mirror of Nature*. Although Rorty later repented of this formulation,[8] in that work he identified truth, at least truth in what he called "normal" discourse, with the agreement of one's cultural peers ("objectivity is agreement"). I shall say a little later how Rorty escapes, or thinks he escapes, the charge of relativism. But it is natural on first meeting this formulation to take it in a relativistic spirit. So taken it says that truth in a language—any language—is determined by what the majority of the speakers of that language would say.

At this point one has to take account of Rorty's distinction between normal and hermeneutic discourse. In *Philosophy and the Mirror of Nature*, the idea was that much discourse is governed by standards on which the speakers of a language are in agreement. In that book (as in his recent *Contingency, Irony, Solidarity*) those standards were compared to an algorithm, that is, to a decision procedure of the kind computers carry out. This is not the only point at which we will see Rorty—in spite of his well-advertised break with analytic philosophy—employing devices which are very similar to the devices employed by analytic philosophers. The appeal to the notion of an algorithm in explaining how it is that certain things are true and certain things are false in the language of a community, even if meant as a metaphor, is a good example of this.

Rorty's picture is that under normal circumstances English speakers do not come into disagreement about a question like

"Are there enough chairs for everybody in the dining room tonight?". The statement that there are enough chairs is, if true, a truth of "normal discourse", and its truth is certified by procedures on which the members of the community are in agreement. If agreement cannot be reached on a question because members of the community hold allegiance to paradigms which are incommensurable, the discourse is "hermeneutic". The best one can do is try to understand the other in such a dispute and to keep the conversation going, according to Rorty. Statements uttered in hermeneutic discourse are true only in an honorific sense; each side in a dispute calls its statements true, but this is just rhetoric designed to persuade the other side to change its allegiance.

Although *Philosophy and the Mirror of Nature* contains brilliant criticisms of the kinds of metaphysics that Rorty rejects, Rorty's positive views are spelled out very elliptically and incompletely. In particular, it is not clear what the notion of agreement of one's cultural peers comes to, apart from the metaphor of an algorithm. If I say to my wife "our kitchen needs painting", the only cultural peer who is aware that I think our kitchen needs painting in this case is my wife (assuming I don't discuss the matter with anyone else). In a sense, my cultural peers agree: that is, all of my cultural peers who actually know that I made the judgment agree it is true. Does that mean the judgment is true? Let us take a more extreme case. Let us suppose that I live alone and I think my kitchen needs painting, and I don't discuss this judgment with anyone. In that case all of my cultural peers who were aware of my judgment (namely me) agree that it is true. Does that mean that it is true, on Rorty's theory?

Most readers of Rorty take him to be saying that a judgment in normal discourse is true just in case one's cultural peers *would agree* if they were present, or if they were informed of the relevant circumstances. But the appeal to counterfactuals is something that Rorty himself has rejected, at least in a paper written after *Philosophy and the Mirror of Nature*.[9] According to Rorty, to appeal to what people who were not actually present would say if they were present is to appeal to "ghost observers". I don't know whether this represents a change of mind on Rorty's part, or whether he already rejected the counterfactual interpretation of his formula when he wrote *Philosophy and the Mirror of Nature*. In the latter case, I don't know how to interpret the formula at all. It seems likely that the metaphor of an algorithm seduced Rorty into assuming that a verification procedure is something which *would* give a result if applied, as a matter of objective "computational" fact, independent of who employs the algorithm. If so, he was unconsciously borrowing a picture from a philosophy which is diametrically opposed to his own.

Since Rorty is too hard to interpret, let us simply imagine a typical relativist who does use counterfactuals unselfconsciously, and who holds that what is true in a culture is determined by what the members of the culture *would say* (if they would fall into irresolvable disagreement, then this relativist may say, like Rorty, that the sentence in question does not belong to "normal discourse", or he may regard it as having no truth value, not even a relative truth value). The very unselfconciousness with which such a relativist uses counterfactuals is the problem. If the truth or falsity of the statement that my kitchen needs painting depends on what my cultural peers would say, then what determines that? What determines what my cultural peers *would* say?

Contemporary analyses of counterfactuals suggest that two things determine it: (1) which possible situations (or which possible worlds) are close to the actual world (or, as I would prefer to say, *relevant to the statement when we consider the actual situation in which it was made*); and (2) what *would happen* in those possible situations. For a physicalist, the latter is no problem: if the possible situations are completely described in the language of physics, say by a "state function" in the sense of quantum mechanics, or of whatever theory may be a successor to quantum mechanics, what will happen in that situation (or the probability that any given thing will happen in that situation) is determined by the laws of fundamental physics (or Fodor might say that it is determined by the laws of fundamental physics plus the laws of the relevant "special sciences").[10] But this account makes the truth value of a counterfactual depend on the notion of something being a law of physics (and/or a law of the special sciences)—not a law of the accepted physics (or, respectively, special sciences) but a law of the true physics (special sciences), whatever that may be—and this is hardly acceptable to a relativist. Even if the notion of truth is itself interpreted relativistically in this formulation, the relativist has a problem: the truth value of the statement that my kitchen needs painting depends (for the relativist) on the truth value of the statement that people (in various hypothetical situations) would say that the paint in my kitchen is dingy and peeling, and that in turn depends on what the relevant laws are (physical, biological, psychological, and so on), and that in turn depends on what people would say the relevant laws are.

Relativists may, of course, deny that they need a "semantics" for counterfactuals. They may just insist that the counterfactual is clear as it stands, and that its truth needs no explanation at all. But metaphysical innocence, like other kinds, once lost is hard to regain. Once one has seen how difficult it is to give an account of the truth of a counterfactual, it is hard to see why someone who regards the truth of ordinary non-counterfactual statements as problematic, as a notion to be given up or radically modified, would regard counterfactual truth as unproblematic.

Let us suppose that our typical relativist does so regard it. At this point he or she encounters the following paradox. It is a fact about our present culture that there is no philosophical unanimity in it: we do not all accept any one philosophy, and certainly we are not all relativists. Moreover, this is likely to continue to be the case for some time. Rorty himself would very likely regard this lack of philosophical unanimity as a very good feature of our culture, and one which he would like to preserve. But if, as a matter of empirical fact, the statement "the majority of my cultural peers would not agree that relativism is correct" is true, then, according to the relativist's own criterion of truth, relativism is not true!

This inconsistency is not a logical inconsistency, because it depends on an empirical premise about the culture, but the empirical premise is one that few people would challenge. Rorty himself would say that his account of truth in *Philosophy and the Mirror of Nature* was not meant to apply to hermeneutic discourse but only to normal discourse. Thus the assertions of both relativism and anti-relativism are not themselves true or false in the sense in which statements in normal discourse are true or false. If I say that a philosophical utterance is true, I am, on Rorty's view, simply "paying it a compliment". To put it in another way, the statement of what sounds like relativism is for Rorty not the announcement of a metaphysical discovery, but a bit of rhetoric: a bit of rhetoric whose purpose is to get us to change our ways, to give up talk of truth and falsity rather than to express some kind of metaphysical truth.[11] Relativism à la Rorty is rhetoric.

Relativism and Solipsism

Typical relativists do think, paradoxically, that they have made some sort of metaphysical discovery. What are they to do if relativism involves a contradiction (or if a contradiction can be derived from relativism using logic that they do not challenge and uncontroversial[12] empirical fact)? The move of "deconstruction" is from relativism to nihilism. Instead of offering a formula which is supposed to tell us what truth is, deconstructionists announce that the notion of truth is incoherent, part of a "metaphysics of presence".[13] Alan Montefiore reported to me that he once heard Derrida say "The concept of truth is inconsistent, but absolutely indispensable!" But what does it mean to say that a concept we find indispensable in daily life is "inconsistent"? Some uses of the word "true" may be inconsistent (as the familiar semantical paradoxes illustrate), but what does it mean to say that *every* use of the word "true" is inconsistent (or that every use of the word "leads us back to" such suspect notions as "presence", "full speech", and so forth)?

The only evidence that French philosophers offer for this astounding claim is that certain *accounts* of truth are, if not inconsistent, at least no longer metaphysically satisfactory. (According to Derrida, even the notion of a signifier—a word with a meaning—"leads us back to or retains us in the logocentric circle".)[14] The collapse of a large number of alternative philosophical accounts of truth is a very different thing from the collapse of the notion of truth itself,[15] just as the collapse of a large number of different philosophical accounts of certainty is a very different thing from the collapse of the ordinary notion of certainty, as Wittgenstein tried to tell us in his last work. When a French philosopher wants to know if the concept of truth, or the concept of a sign, or the concept of referring, is consistent or not he proceeds by looking at Aristotle, Plato, Nietzsche, and Heidegger, and not by looking at how the words "true", "sign", "refer" are used. But this shows us more about French philosophy than it does about truth, signs, or reference.

What is interesting is that there is a way of making relativism consistent which was once more or less popular in philosophy, at least in disguised forms, and which is no longer popular at all: first-person relativism. If I am a relativist, and I define truth as what *I* agree with, or as what I would agree with if I investigated long enough, then, as long as I continue to agree with my own definition of truth, the argument that my position faces a standpoint problem, or is self-refuting, does not immediately arise. First-person relativism is virtually unfindable on today's philosophical scene, and it may be worthwhile to ask ourselves why.

One reason, a superficial but important one, is the widespread attention, even if not always accompanied by comprehension, that has been paid to Wittgenstein's private language argument. The private language argument is certainly difficult to understand, but part of its thrust is uncontroversial; what Wittgenstein might say, if he were addressing a relativist of the kind just described, would be something like this: "You speak as if language were your invention, subject to your will at each moment. The language games we play are alterable by our will only to a very limited extent. They are cultural formations, which have an enormous amount of inertia. Rightness and wrongness in a language game is internal to that language game; it's not something that was invented by you, and it's not something that refers to you." A language game, Wittgenstein tells us, "consists of the recurrent procedures of that game in time".[16] The procedures in question existed long before me, and will continue to exist long after me.

Now, in one sense, it might be said that this is not an argument. (I don't pretend, of course, to have summarized the private language argument here.)[17] The first-person relativist might say that even in natural language we sometimes speak of things as if they were non-relative which we later discover are relative. We do not ordinarily say that two events are simultaneous or non-simultaneous *relative to my frame*; yet, after learning of the special theory of relativity, we know that simultaneity is in fact relative to a frame, although there are good reasons why it is not necessary to take account of this in ordinary contexts. Similarly, the first-person relativist might claim to have made a philosophical discovery that truth, as we ordinarily speak of it in natural language, refers to a relational property. It is true that that relational property doesn't presuppose the relativist's own existence: when you speak, truth is truth relative to you; and when John speaks, truth is truth relative to John; and when Joan speaks, truth is truth relative to Joan; and so on.

The reason people don't take this line, I think, is that it is simply not convincing as a description of the way we use the word "true". If I hear someone say that palladium is a rare earth, I do not take the assertion to mean that the speaker would believe that palladium is a rare earth if he or she investigated long enough (what's that to me, after all?). I take the speaker to be making an assertion that is to be checked—by us or by a third party—by studying palladium. It could of course be that after we have looked at palladium we will still not be able to agree on whether the assertion was right. But the language game of classifying elements in this way could not function at all if in every case we were unable to come into agreement on whether something was a rare earth.

Mary Warnock once said that Sartre gave us not arguments or proofs but "a description so clear and vivid that when I think of his description and fit it to my own case, I cannot fail to see its application". It seems to me that this is a very good description of what Wittgenstein was doing, not just in the private language argument, but over and over again in his work. Suppose we simply *describe* how we use the word "true" carefully and attentively, suppose we give its "phenomenology". We will find that the idea that it stands for the property of "being what I would believe if I continued to investigate" simply wrong.

I don't think that the private language argument, influential as it is, is the only reason for the decline of first-person relativism. Solipsism has never been a popular philosophical position, and first-person relativism sounds dangerously close to solipsism. Indeed, it is not clear how it can avoid being solipsism. [18]

Consider, for example, a statement about a human being who is no longer alive, a statement whose truth value we are no longer in a position to determine, say, "Caesar was shaved on the day he crossed the Rubicon". It is part of what Cavell has called our "acknowledgment" of other human beings that we treat statements that *they* are able to verify as having just as much right to be called meaningful and true (or false) as statements that we ourselves are able to verify. If a statement is such that *no* human being could ever, under any conceivable circumstances, verify it, then, indeed, we begin to wonder—or some of us begin to wonder—whether the statement even *has* a truth value; but the statement that Caesar had a shave on the day that he crossed the Rubicon is one that at least one human being, namely Julius Caesar himself, was in a perfectly good position to verify. I no more doubt that that statement has a truth value than I do that the statement that I shaved this morning has a truth value. For a relativist, however—and now it doesn't make any difference whether we mean a first-person relativist or a cultural relativist—it is very likely that the statement about Julius Caesar has no truth value. It may very well be the case, in fact it probably is the case, that all traces of that event or non-event have long ago been obliterated. Worse, the question of whether it does have a truth value is just a question about what the relativist (in the case of first-person relativists) or the culture (in the case of cultural relativists) will come to believe, if they do their best (by their own lights, or those of the culture) to investigate the question. Julius Caesar is a logical construction out of the actual and potential beliefs of present-day people, on such a story.

Coming back to first-person relativism, what is true of Julius Caesar is true of people who are alive now. If you and I are not the first-person relativist in question, then the truth about me and about you and about the friends and the spouse of the first-person relativist is, for the first-person relativist, simply a function of his or her own dispositions to believe. This is why first-person relativism sounds like thinly disguised solipsism. But it is hard to see why cultural relativism is any better off, in this respect. Is solipsism with a "we" any better than solipsism with an "I"?

Materialism, Relativism, Metaphysical Realism

Wittgenstein introduced the image of language as an overlapping system of games. But what is often overlooked is that in one place Wittgenstein stresses that *rightness or wrongness in a language game is not always determined by rules.* I shall discuss the passage in question later; for the moment let me just say that the passage we will examine[19] also makes a different and less emphasized point. Wittgenstein looks at disagreements about what is going on in the soul of another human being (Is he faking an emotion? Has she fallen in love?). Sometimes such a disagreement can be settled to everybody's satisfaction. But Wittgenstein describes a case which is not so settled, and where what counts is "unwägbare Evidenz" (imponderable evidence).

The phenomenon of the *controversial,* of what cannot be settled to the satisfaction of everyone who is "linguistically competent", is, however, ubiquitous, and extends far beyond the psychological. Even so-called factual judgments are frequently controversial, at least in some parts of the culture—

(think of the disputes about evolution between scientists and fundamentalists, or think of the impossibility of convincing some people that there are no American prisoners of war left in Vietnam). It is part of our form of life, part of the way we live and think and act and will go on living and thinking and acting, that each of us treats many controversial propositions as definitely having a truth value. Rorty will of course say that such sentences are not part of "normal" discourse, that to call them true is only to "pay them a compliment"; but the minute he leaves his study he will talk of the fundamentalist opponent of evolution, or the right-wing crank who thinks that there are prisoners of war in Vietnam, as a fool. What it is right to say in a given context cannot always be established to everyone's satisfaction; but it is nonetheless the right thing to say.

Yet the explicit recognition that language games are human activities in which what is right and wrong is not simply conventional, is not simply determined by consensus, but is something that requires evaluation, is troubling to many a contemporary sensibility.[20] (Perhaps it was even troubling to Wittgenstein; perhaps this is why in the *Investigations* there is only this one isolated reference to this all-important fact.[21] Later I shall talk about some unpublished lectures of Wittgenstein, which were taken down by others and published after his death, which shed more light on the nature of his thinking.) But the distrust of the normative in present-day philosophy is evidenced above all by the lengths to which philosophers will go to avoid admitting that truth—that is, the rightness of what is said—*is* a normative notion.[22]

We have seen that both materialists and relativists avail themselves of the counterfactual conditional when they try to explain what truth is. At first blush, one would not expect either kind of philosopher to be very happy with this way of talking. Matters of fact about non-actual situations do not fit very well into either the worldview of materialism or the anti-metaphysical prejudices of relativism. If, in spite of this, one finds both kinds of philosophers resorting to this machinery, it can be only because the price of not doing so seems too high. Philosophers of a more traditional kind would have tried to escape the problem in still another way. For such philosophers, to say that a sentence is true is not to make a normative judgment at all: it is just to say that the sentence "agrees" with something ("the facts") or that it "corresponds" to something ("a state of affairs"). But I have shown elsewhere, using a number of theorems from contemporary model theory,[23] that the notion of "correspondence" is totally empty in this context. It is possible, in fact, to interpret our language, in the sense of "interpret" used in contemporary model theory, in such a way that the sentences of any consistent theory "agree with reality" under an appropriate correspondence. Even if the truth conditions for all the sentences of our language are in some way fixed, it is still possible to find a correspondence under which every sentence of our language retains its present truth conditions (up to logical equivalence), although the references of the individual words are changed so radically that the word "cherry" ends up referring to cats and the word "mat" ends up referring to trees.[24] It was in response to this theorem that a number of physicalist philosophers suggested that what singles out the reference of a term is not a matter of model theoretic correspondence in the abstract, but specifically of "causal connection" or "causal attachment". In the previous chapter I examined the most recent form of this suggestion and saw how little it actually comes to. Beyond that, as I have also pointed out, these philosophers ignore the language dependence of the ordinary notion of causality itself. In effect, the ordinary notion of causality is a *cognitive* notion, and these philosophers treat it as if it were a purely physical one.

What I have been suggesting is that philosophy of language is in a bind because it is hell-bent on eliminating the normative in favor of something else, however problematic that something else may be. In analytic philosophy, this desire to eliminate the normative often goes hand-in-hand with the idea that science is "value free" and that science and only science tells us how things "really are". In the next chapter I examine this science-ethics distinction in Bernard Williams' recent and influential *Ethics and the Limits of Philosophy.*

5

Bernard Williams and the Absolute Conception of the World

Bernard Williams is one of the most influential British philosophers, and deservedly so, considering his brilliance, his erudition, his wit, and his involvement in public affairs. In *Ethics and the Limits of Philosophy* and *Descartes: The Project of Pure Enquiry*[1] he tries to win us over to a metaphysically materialist view of the world, while recognizing that the sort of reduction of the intentional to the non-intentional that Fodor and Millikan hope to achieve is impossible. At the same time he tries to achieve a reconciliation of relativism and a weak form of cognitivism,[2] by exploiting the Kuhnian idea of incommensurability.[3] Given the ambition of these two books and the distinction of the author, I believe that it will be well worth while to examine his doctrines here.

Although I shall be interested in seeing how a successor to the fact-value dichotomy, if not the traditional fact-value dichotomy itself, makes an appearance in Bernard Williams' philosophy, I shall begin with Williams' metaphysics, because that metaphysics—and especially his notion of an "absolute conception of the world"—is at the base of all of his arguments.

The Absolute Conception and the Metaphor of Perspectives

The notion of an "absolute conception of the world" as something that science ideally converges on (and ethics does not, even ideally) is employed in the closing chapters of *Ethics and the Limits of Philosophy.*[4] Thus, Williams writes,

> The basic idea behind the distinction between the scientific and the ethical, expressed in terms of convergence, is very simple. In a scientific inquiry there should ideally be convergence on an answer, where the best explanation of the convergence involves the idea that the answer represents how things are; in the area of the ethical, at least at a high level of generality, there is no such coherent hope. The distinction does not turn on any difference in whether convergence will actually occur, and it is important that this is not what the argument is about. The point of the contrast is that, even if this happens, it will not be correct to think it has come about because convergence has been guided by how things actually are, whereas convergence in the sciences might be explained in that way if it does happen. (p. 136)

And again,

> In reflecting on the world that is there *anyway*, independent of our experience, we must concentrate not in the first instance on what our beliefs are about, but on how they represent what they are about. We can select among our beliefs and features of our world pictures some that we can reasonably claim to represent the world in a way to the maximum degree independent of our perspective and its peculiarities. The resultant picture of things, if we can carry through this task, can be called the "absolute conception" of the world. In terms of that conception, we may hope to explain the possibility of attaining the conception itself, and also the possibility of other, perspectival, conceptions.
>
> The notion of an absolute conception can serve to make effective a distinction between "the world as it is independent of our experience" and "the world as it seems to us." It does this by understanding "the world as it seems to us" as "the world as it seems peculiarly to us"; the absolute conception

(what does this claim consist in?)

will, correspondingly, be a conception of the world that might
be arrived at by any investigators, even if they were very
different from us . . . The aim is to outline the possibility of
a convergence characteristic of science, one that could mean-
ingfully be said to be a convergence on how things (anyway)
are. (pp. 138–139)

The notion is explained more completely in Williams' earlier
Descartes.[5] Like Descartes, Williams accepts a sharp distinction
between "primary" qualities (such as extension, but in present-
day physics also mass, charge, the various field intensities and
so on) and "secondary" qualities (such as heat and green). In
principle, what Williams calls an "absolute" description (or
"conception") of the world can be given using terms for the
primary qualities alone.[6] And only such a description describes
the world as it is independent of our experience, as opposed to
describing how it is in relation to one or another tribe or species
of observers.

In *Descartes*, Williams introduces these ideas by means of a
thought experiment. We are invited to consider how we would
describe the world *before* there were observers, or, alternatively,
to imagine the world as it might be if there were not any
observers.[7] In a colloquial description, we might, of course,
include secondary qualities in our account, speaking of green
grass or a hot day, but we are aware, or can easily be brought
to be aware (Williams claims), that in so doing we are simply
describing how the grass *would have appeared to observers* with
our sort of visual apparatus if they had been present, or how
the day *would have felt to observers* with our sort of body. This
information is not really necessary, nor is it appropriate if we
want to describe the world without observers as it is independent
of our experience. Thus we come to see that this world, the
world without observers, can be described (as it is independent
of our experience) in terms of primary qualities alone.

Williams' motive for introducing the absolute conception in this way is the following, I believe: the world we live in, the world *with* observers, evolved out of a world without observers. And the laws that govern our world are just the laws that governed the world without observers. So a description of our world using just the primary qualities that we need to describe the world without observers *must* be possible. The seductive appeal of this thought is undeniable. But is the thought really right?

Consider the following: it is true that with the evolution of animals and human beings and the development of human (and animal) societies no new *physical* laws came into existence. Very few people any longer suppose that living things violate any laws of physics (as some thinkers supposed as late as the nineteenth century), or that human beings have immaterial souls which cause them to move in ways that violate the laws governing the conservation of momentum,[8] as Descartes' model required. Physics can, in principle, predict the probability with which a human body will follow any given trajectory, given appropriate initial data, as it can predict the probability with which anything else will follow any given trajectory. But such predictions are of phenomena which are described in the language of physics, not the language of biology, psychology, or economics. With the appearance of living things and societies new laws *do* appear; not laws which contradict the laws of physics, but laws which apply to things under descriptions which are not available in physics. The laws of economics are a good example. "Supply" and "demand" cannot even be defined in the language of physics; so the question of "explaining the relation between supply and demand" is not a meaningful question to address to a physicist.

Williams is perfectly well aware of this consideration, and his reply involves an extended use of a particular metaphor—a metaphor which appears repeatedly in both of the books I alluded to. This is the metaphor of *perspective*. In optics, it is clear what we would mean by an "objective description" of a scene: namely, a description of the sizes and shapes and locations of all the bodies in the scene and of the sources of light. Using this objective description, and the laws of optics, which we may think of as a part of the objective description, we can predict how the scene will look "in perspective" from any particular given point of view, such as why Ermintrude looks tiny to Elmer when Elmer is looking down at her from the top of a hill, and why Elmer looks tiny to Ermintrude at the same moment. In this sense, the objective description *explains* all the "local perspectives".

Williams' leading idea is that the descriptions we give using the vocabularies of the special sciences, using terms for secondary qualities, using ordinary-language intentional terms,[9] and so forth, can *in a strictly analogous way* be explained using the "absolute conception"; using, that is to say, not present-day physics, but an envisaged perfected analogue of present-day physics.[10]

The metaphor is carried even further. In the optical case, the objective description is one that the various observers can agree on (if they make the appropriate measurements, confirm the laws of optics, and so on), even if their perspectival descriptions appear to disagree. In a strictly analogous way, Williams believes that any conceivable species of intelligent beings (if they frame hypotheses properly, perform the appropriate experiments) can "converge" toward agreement on the laws of the ideal physics, in the fashion first envisaged by C. S. Peirce.[11] (This does not mean that they can ever be sure that they *have* converged on the absolute conception, however; this is not required for us to be able to employ the absolute conception, Williams assures us.)[12] Williams allows that the optical case is disanalogous in only one way; he believes that humans can, when we get sufficiently close to it, use the absolute conception to explain the possibility of our local conceptions (including our grasp of the absolute conception itself), but, puzzlingly, he does not insist that *all* the other species of observers must be able to do this as well.[13] The reasons for this breakdown of the analogy will be be discussed later.

The Entanglement of Fact and Value

It must be emphasized that, in Williams' view, to deny that something is part of the "absolute conception of the world" is not necessarily to deny that it is true or that it can be knowledge. It is *true* that the grass is green, and we *know* that the grass is green; but this, although genuine knowledge, is not knowledge of how things are "independent of perspective"—rather, it is knowledge of how things are in our local perspective. And the same goes for ethical statements. Williams does not deny that ethical utterances have a truth value, nor does he deny that there can be ethical knowledge. (In the jargon of contemporary philosophy, Williams is not a "non-cognitivist".) I am not entirely sure of the reasons for Williams' rejection of non-cognitivism, but one reason is surely an increased appreciation of what might be called the entanglement of fact and value.[14] That entanglement was a constant theme in the writings of John Dewey, whose views I will turn to later. But this aspect of pragmatism was neglected in Anglo-American philosophy after Dewey's death, in spite of Morton White's valiant effort to keep it alive in *Reunion in Philosophy,* and it was, perhaps, Iris Murdoch who reopened the theme in a very different way.

Three essays by Murdoch, published together as *The Sovereignty of "Good",* contain a large number of valuable insights and remarks: two have proved especially influential. Murdoch

was one of the first English-speaking philosophers[15] to emphasize that languages have two very different sorts of ethical concepts: abstract ethical concepts (Williams calls them "thin" ethical concepts), such as *good* and *right*, and more descriptive,
less abstract concepts (Williams calls them "thick" ethical concepts), such as *cruel, pert, inconsiderate, chaste*. Murdoch (and
later, and in a more spelled-out way, John McDowell)[16] argued
that there is no way of saying what the "descriptive component"
of the meaning of a word like "cruel" or "inconsiderate" is
without using a word of the same kind; as McDowell put the
argument, a word has to be connected to a certain set of
"evaluative interests" in order to function the way such a thick
ethical word functions, and the speaker has to be aware of those
interests and be able to identify imaginatively with them in
order to apply the word to novel cases or circumstances in the
way a sophisticated speaker of the language would.

For example, someone who has studied how the word "cruel"
is used without performing such an act of imaginative identification could predict that the word would be used in certain
obvious cases, for instance, torture. But such a person would
be baffled by the fact that some cases which seemed (from the
same external point of view) to be cases of "kindness" would be
described by us as "subtle forms of cruelty", and by the fact
that some cases of what he or she would describe as cruelty
would be described by us as "not cruel at all under the circumstances". The attempt of non-cognitivists to split words like
"cruel" into a "descriptive meaning component" and a "pre-
scriptive meaning component" founders on the impossibility of
saying what the "descriptive meaning" is without using the word
"cruel" itself, or a synonym.

Murdoch also emphasized that when we are actually confronted with situations requiring ethical evaluation, whether or
not they also require some action on our part, the sorts of

descriptions that we need—descriptions of the motives and character of human beings, above all—are in the language of a "sensitive novelist", not in scientistic or bureaucratic jargon. When a situation or a person or a motive is appropriately described, the decision as to whether something is good or bad or right or wrong frequently follows automatically. For example, our evaluation of a person's moral stature may critically depend on whether we describe the person as "impertinent" or "unstuffy". Our life-world, Murdoch is telling us, does not factor neatly into "facts" and "values"; we live in a messy human world in which seeing reality with all its nuances—seeing it as George Eliot, or Flaubert, or Henry James, or Murdoch herself, can to some extent teach us to see it—and making appropriate "value judgments" are simply not separable abilities.

Williams not only considers these views correct, or likely to be correct, but in fact elaborates on them in an interesting way. Under the influence of quasi-social-scientific, quasi-philosophical talk about "facts" and "value judgements" many people simply assume that if we praise somebody we must, implicitly at least, avail ourselves of some "thin" (highly abstract) ethical notion such as good/bad or right/wrong. Thus, if we learn that, in a traditional society, Elder Jones criticized Matilda by saying she was not chaste, we are likely to analyze what Elder Jones was saying as follows:

(1) Matilda is not [insert a "value-neutral" word with the same descriptive meaning as "chaste"] (factual claim).
(2) It is bad not to be [insert the same "value-neutral" term here] (value judgment).
(3) Matilda is bad (unstated value conclusion).

According to Williams, however, it is quite unwarranted to attribute our own abstract ethical notions in this way to every society on the face of the earth. [17] Williams performs the thought experiment of imagining a "hypertraditional society" which lacks our thin ethical concepts altogether, but which still possesses thick ethical concepts[18] (imagine Elder Jones and Matilda live in such a hypertraditional society). Williams believes that a thick ethical concept like "chaste" can function as *both* a description and a value judgment, and it is a fallacy of division to suppose that the whole speech act must be divisible into a descriptive claim (which could, in principle, be expressed in value-neutral language) and a value judgment (which could, in principle, be expressed using thin ethical concepts).[19]

Murdoch's second claim, that we cannot in fact do without our thick ethical language and the point of view that goes with it, is one that Williams would heartily endorse. (He would rephrase it by saying that we cannot do without our "local perspective".)

Relativism and the Fact-Value Dichotomy

According to Bernard Williams, a properly worked-out "non-objectivism", by which he means a position which rejects the characteristic thesis of relativism (that propositions are "true for" or "false for" one or another culture, rather than simply true or false) while finding a "truth in relativism", can do justice to the way in which fact and value can be inseparable—do justice to the way some statements which are both descriptive and true ("Caligula was a mad tyrant") can also be value judgments. It can do this by exploiting the distinction between truth and absoluteness.

Williams nowhere explains what he understands truth to be, but he obviously intends it to include right-assertability in the local language game, so that if the practices and shared values of a culture determine an established use for the word "chaste" (a use which is sufficiently definite to permit speakers to come to agreement on someone's chastity or lack of chastity), then it can be simply true that a person in the culture is chaste. Of course, if we do not belong to the culture in question and do not share the relevant evaluative interests, then we will not describe the person in question as chaste, even if we know that that is a correct thing to say in that culture; we will be "disbarred" from using the word, as Williams puts it. As he also puts it (with deliberate paradox), that So-and-so is chaste is possible knowledge for someone in the culture, but not possible knowledge for *us*. Note that Williams does not say that "So-and-so is chaste" is *true for* Elder Jones' and Matilda's culture but not *true for*, say, the culture of some Berkeley Free Love Movement. Williams argues that that sort of relativism quickly leads to absurdity ("I know where you're coming from, but, you know, *relativism just isn't true for me*").[20]

Nevertheless, whether it is possible knowledge for us or not, on Williams' view, "Matilda is chaste" can be true in the very same sense in which "snow is white" is true, while still being an ethical utterance. But there *is* an insight in non-cognitivism, Williams claims, even if non-cognitivism was mistaken in what it took to be its essential thesis, that ethical sentences are not capable of truth (or, alternatively, that an ethical sentence has a distinct "value component", and this "value component" is not capable of truth). But what *was* the insight that the fact-value distinction tried to capture?

According to Williams, there are truths and truths. If I say that grass is green, for example, I certainly speak the truth; but I do not speak what he calls the *absolute* truth. I do not describe the world as it is "anyway", independent of any and every "perspective". As I have explained, Williams thinks that the concept "green" (and possibly the concept "grass" as well) are not concepts that finished science would use to describe the properties that things have apart from any "local perspective".

[handwritten margin note: ethical value judgment— secondary qualities]

[handwritten note at bottom: non-cogn. - ethical sentences - don't have absolute-truth values]

Martians or Alpha Centaurians, for example, might not have the sorts of eyes we have. They would not recognize any such property as "green", and "grass" may be too unscientific a classification to appear in their finished science. Only concepts that would appear in the (final) description of the world that any species of determined natural researchers is destined to converge on belong to the "absolute conception of the world". The philosophically important point here is that while value judgments containing thick ethical concepts can be true, they cannot be absolute. The world, as it is "independent of our experience", is *cold*. Values (like colors) are projected onto the world, not discovered in it.

A second important point is that, on Williams' view, values are even worse off than colors in this respect, for the discovery that green is a secondary quality has not undermined our ability to use the word. Although we no longer think that colors are non-dispositional properties of external things, this in no way affects the utility of color classification. But the realization that value attributes, even "thick" ones ("chaste", "cruel", "pert"), are projections has a tendency to cause us to lose our ability to use those terms. If we become reflective to too great a degree, if we absorb too much of the absolute conception of the world, we will no longer be able to employ our ethical concepts. The realization that ethical concepts are projections places us in a ticklish position: we cannot stop being reflective, but we cannot afford to be *too* reflective. We are in an unstable equilibrium.

The reason for this difference between ordinary secondary qualities like green and thick ethical attributes like chastity, according to Williams, is that the interests which color classification subserves are fixed by our biology (according to Williams) and thus are universal among human beings, whereas the interests that thick ethical concepts subserve are the interests of one human community (one "social world") or another. But the interests which define one social world may be in conflict with the interests which define a different social world. Realizing that our ethical descriptions are in this way parochial (however "true" they may also be) can unsettle us, weaken our confidence in our own ethical language.

Williams believes that coming to realize just how far ethical description misses describing the world as it is "absolutely" must affect our first-order ethical judgments. According to him, moral praise or condemnation of another way of life loses all point when that other way of life is too distant from ours (too distant in the sense that neither way of life is a live option for the other). It makes no sense to try to evaluate the way of life of a medieval Samurai, or of a bronze age society. To ask whether their ways of life were right or their judgments true is (or should be) impossible for us; "the question of appraisal does not genuinely arise",[21] once we understand the non-absoluteness of ethical discourse. That the question lapses is "the truth in relativism". (Accepting this view is what Williams calls "taking a relativist view" of such conflicts; note that this is different from accepting the kind of relativism that I discussed earlier.)

This is undoubtedly an ambitious and interesting set of views. Let us now examine them critically, beginning with the notion of "absoluteness".

What Is "Absoluteness"?

Earlier I quoted two representative passages from *Ethics and the Limits of Philosphy* in which Williams explains what he means by the "absolute conception", as well as briefly summarizing his explanations in *Descartes*. In all these explanations, three features recur, with different emphasis in different places:

(1) The primary qualities (which describe the world as it is

"anyway", independent of experience) do not depend on our constitution, whereas the secondary qualities "depend on psychological factors" (*Descartes*, p. 241).

(2) The absolute conception (which is equated with the complete description of the world in terms of primary qualities) explains the possibility of the local conceptions, and its own possibility. It (ideally) includes "a theory of knowledge and of error" (*Descartes*, p. 246).

(3) If science succeeds in converging on the absolute conception, that convergence is explained by the fact that that is "how things (anyway) are".

The first feature, the "dependence on psychological factors" of the secondary qualities, seems obvious to Williams, although it is nowhere explained very clearly. Here is one discussion:

> A familiar line is to treat "——— is green" as in fact relational, though complexly and hypothetically so, equivalent roughly to "——— is of such a nature as to look green to standard observers in standard circumstances". Under such an analysis, ascriptions of secondary qualities will in fact mention human relativities . . . it will be clear both why and how secondary qualities should be laid aside in giving the conception of the world as it is without observers. However this relational way of analysing secondary qualities . . . may well not be correct. For one thing, it leaves us with the discouraging task of explaining "——— looks green" in some way which does not presuppose any prior understanding of "——— is green". How the relational pattern of analysis might possibly be replaced is part of a larger question, how the partial views and local experiences are themselves to be related to the world as conceived in independence of them.
> (*Descartes*, p. 244)

Unfortunately, far from giving us a reason for agreeing that secondary qualities should be "laid aside", this passage *rejects* one of the common reasons for thinking so. Williams also tells us that "the traditional arguments bring out the ways in which the secondary qualities depend on psychological factors" (p. 241), by explaining why things should seem one color to one person and a different color to another. But we have, in fact, perfectly good ways of deciding what the color of, say, a surface is (for example, by comparing it with color samples); and if a red surface looks gray to a color-blind person (or "monochrome" to a species without color vision), that does not show that the color is relative to the viewer, but only that some viewers make mistakes (and some species lack color vision). Indeed, the tendency to confuse a secondary quality with the sensation of the secondary quality appears throughout these pages (237ff). Thus, Williams quotes with approval the traditional argument that heat cannot be physical because it shades insensibly into pain (p. 237), an argument which transparently conflates heat (temperature) and the *sensation* of heat.

The example of heat is interesting because its scientific counterpart, temperature,[22] has been identified by physics with an *objective* property of things, albeit a highly disjunctive one, one which figures in the most fundamental physical theories (for instance, in quantum field theory, the notion of the temperature of the field is an important one). Perhaps Williams' point is that an ordinary-language predicate like "hot" presupposes a standard which is based partly on our physiology and partly on contextual interests, in short on what Democritus called "convention". This may be granted, and it may be granted that, for that reason, a precise description which abstracts from that physiology and those interests would replace predicates like "hot", "lukewarm", and "cold" with numerically specified temperatures; but that does not mean that "heat" (temperature) is not a feature of the objective world. Moreover, in the case of color, Williams' picture is clearly that there is no such thing

color, heat depend on s.o. perceiving them

in the world (Williams speaks of "such large-scale mistakes as that the world is itself colored", *Descartes*, p. 249). Does Williams also think that it is a "large-scale mistake" to think that some parts of the world are *hotter* than other parts?

Perhaps Williams thinks that the notion of heat in our common language (the language that Wilfrid Sellars referred to as "the manifest image of the world") just *doesn't refer to the same thing* as the scientific notion of temperature. But this "two worlds" view is hardly forced on us by science itself; why shouldn't we say that science has discovered what the layman is talking about, *discovered what being hotter and colder is,* rather than saying that science has discovered that there are no hot or cold bodies in the world?

We would, indeed, have a good reason for saying that the layman is wrong about the world if we were to attribute to the layman the idea that his sensation of heat (or "idea" of heat, in seventeenth-century philosophical parlance) "resembles" the heat in the world; but this argument would equally support the idea that there is no *distance* in the world: the layman's sensation (or "idea") of distance hardly "resembles" the distance talked about by the relativistic physicist or the supergravitation theorist. Thomas Reid already objected to attributing to laymen this confusion between heat and the sensation of heat, and Williams himself criticizes some seventeenth-century thinkers for arguing in this way (pp. 240–241).

Can we say, at least, that the sensation of heat cannot be identified with anything in an objective physical description of the world? To do so would require arguing that sensations cannot be identical with brain processes (which *are* part of the absolute conception of the world), and this is not a task which Williams anywhere undertakes.

Finally, Williams might fall back on the claim that the predicates "hot", "green", and so on are at least not *synonymous* with any terms in the absolute conception (even if they share reference with them); but this would hardly be a very interesting claim, even if we assume that the notion of synonymy is sufficiently clear. Donald Davidson has suggested in a famous essay that a very similar claim is *not* sufficiently clear: "Suppose that in my office of Minister of Scientific Language I want the new man to stop using words that refer, say, to feelings, thoughts, and intentions and to talk instead of the physiological states and happenings that are assumed to be more or less identical with the mental riff and raff. How do I tell if my advice has been heeded if the new man speaks a new language? For all I know, the shiny new phrases, although stolen from the old language in which they refer to physiological stirrings, may in his mouth play the role of the messy old mental concepts" (*Inquiries into Truth and Interpretation*, p. 188).

Nor is the situation much better if we consider color rather than heat. Although the philosopher Larry Hardin[23] has argued on the basis of contemporary theories that color is "subjective", I believe that most researchers hold that color is an objective property, at least in the case of surfaces. For example, the neurobiologist Jerome Lettvin has pointed out[24] that the eye corrects for enormous differences in the chromatic composition of the light shining on objects in the course of the day, and, in doing so, it functions as a "computer" (he has analyzed the "computation" it carries out). It turns out that what the eye provides is a very good estimate (under a wide range of conditions) of certain *objective* potentialities (reflectancies) of the surfaces in question. Color vision is not a mere reaction of our physiology, uncorrelated to anything objective in the surface scanned.

One argument used by Hardin for regarding color as subjective is that the physical property of the surface is highly disjunctive; many different combinations of reflectancies will produce, say, a green surface. But, as Jonathan Westphal points out in a brilliant book on this topic,[25] the disjunction admits of a fairly simple approximate characterization: a surface is green just in case it *refuses* to reflect a significant percentage of red light relative to light of the other colors, including green. The characterization certainly leaves the boundaries fuzzy, but it explains why many different combinations of reflectancies will result in a green surface. Moreover, the argument from disjunctiveness is unpersuasive; temperature is certainly disjunctively defined in present-day physics, but no physicist would regard temperature as "not in the world". Indeed, since any non-disjunctive predicate can be rendered disjunctive (and vice versa) by changing which terms we take as primitive,[26] is it clear that regarding disjunctiveness as a proof that a predicate is not really an objective "universal", as some philosophers do, is not importing a "local perspective", the perspective of a familiar set of linguistic habits, into questions of metaphysics?

Another argument used by Hardin is that judgments as to what is a *standard* green (as opposed to, say, a yellowish green or a bluish green) are not intersubjectively stable. This certainly does show that, unless we adopt a convention, such as a color chart which makes such determinations, there is no fact of the matter as to the "center" of the green part of the spectrum; but it hardly follows that there are no clear cases of green or no clear cases of non-green.

These questions are obviously too hard to settle now. But it should be clear that they are extremely complicated, and the view that green is a perfectly good property of things, one which is relational in the sense of involving the relations of the surface to *light*, but not relational in the sense of involving the relations of the surface to *people*, is still alive and well. Of course, the boundaries of "green" need to be suitably legislated if we are to use it in a precise description of the world without observers; but, as Wheeler et al. point out,[27] "one second" (substitute your favorite unit of time) is not perfectly precisely defined, and indeed never will be. Williams would presumably not regard the fact that the time words of ordinary language have to be made more precise if they are to be used in science as showing that there is a "large-scale mistake" in supposing that events take time; by parity of reasoning, I do not see that the fact that the color words of ordinary language have to be made more precise if they are to be used in science shows that it is a "large-scale mistake" to suppose that the world is colored.

Westphal's explanation of the nature of green, which I have just summarized, identifies green with a *dispositional* property—the disposition to reflect very little red light relative to the proportion of light of other colors which is reflected. It has occurred to me that Williams might now argue that talk of dispositions is also too "perspectival" to figure in the absolute conception. My own arguments in the previous chapters might be used to support such a claim. But again the issues quickly become murky. What I argued is that counterfactuals (and dispositional statements) presuppose a distinction between hypothetical situations which are relevant to the statement's truth or falsity and possible worlds which are not, and such a distinction cannot be drawn in non-normative terms. But to conclude that dispositions are, therefore, "perspectival" would be to assume as a premise just what Williams wants to derive as the *conclusion* of his discussion: that normative notions (such as "relevance") cannot appear in the absolute conception of the world.

relevance can't be expressed in non-norm. terms

Williams argues that "in understanding, even sketchily, at a general and reflective level, why things appear variously colored to various observers, we shall find that we have left behind any idea that, in some way which transcends those facts, they 'really' have one color rather than another". Lettvin's work, and the work that Westphal discusses, may refute this claim.

Williams might reply that even if the color of a surface did turn out to be an objective reflectance property, this still would not effect the contrast he wants to draw between color properties and value properties. But it does not require Williams' elaborate metaphysical story to point out that valuation does not arise from an organ like the eye. (John Dewey, to whose philosophy I turn in the final chapter, would urge that we see valuation as arising from the *criticism of modes of problem solving*.)[28]

The second feature of Williams' argument—that the absolute conception (which is equated with the complete description of the world in terms of primary qualities) explains the possibility of the local conceptions and its own possibility by (ideally) including "a theory of knowledge and of error"—is qualified virtually out of existence in Williams' text almost as soon as it is advanced. For this reason, this feature cannot be the *defining* feature of what Williams calls "absoluteness", although it is absolutely essential to the metaphor of "perspectives".

J. L. Austin once said of the ways of philosophers, "There's the bit where he says it and the bit where he takes it back." Here's the bit where Williams says it:

> This conception of the world must make it possible to explain how it can exist. This conception is not something transcendental, but is an historical product of consciousness in the world, and it must at least yield a comprehension of men and other rational creatures as capable of achieving that conception. (*Descartes*, p. 246)

And here's the bit where he takes it back:

> The demand [that we show the possibility of explanations of the place in the world of "cultural phenomena such as the

local non-absolute conceptions of the world, and of the absolute conception itself, including in that the possibility of physical science"] may be much harder to meet, or to evade. The requirement was that we should be able to overcome relativism in our view of reality through having a view of the world (or at least the coherent conception of such a view) which contains a theory of error; which can explain the existence of rival views, and of itself. But this conception involves a dimension not just of physical explanation, but of social explanation as well. We have to explain the emergence of physical science as something which is indeed knowledge. This entails, if we are to sustain the realist outlook which is essential to the idea of the absolute conception, that physical theory and the interpretation of nature not suffer from the same indeterminacy that may affect translation and the interpretation of the mental. We have to explain, further, how psychological, social and other theories, and also less theoretical views of the world, can be related to the world as we understand it in terms of physical theory. In these philosophical and social scientific tasks, we are not only explaining, but ourselves giving examples of theories which . . . deal with just the kind of subject matter which may be subject to radical indeterminacy of interpretation.

In face of such considerations, the most ambitious ideas that have been entertained of the absolute conception must fail: the idea, for example, of a convergent, self-vindicating unified science of man and nature. How much less than this positivist fantasy [sic] will do? What is the minimum? Perhaps just this: that we should be able to make sense of how natural science can be absolute knowledge of reality, and of why we cannot even agree how much else is absolute knowledge of reality. (*Descartes*, pp. 301–302)

The problem Williams faces is quite simple: the only sense in which the absolute conception, which we are to think of on the model of "physics and natural science", can "explain the possibility of the local conceptions, and its own possibility" is that it can *predict* that certain marks and noises will occur. But this is not to explain how those marks and noises are conceptions or to explain how they describe anything, even "perspectivally".

The problem Williams faces is similar to the problem Wilfrid Sellars, whose views in many ways anticipated Williams' present views, notoriously faced. Like Williams, Sellars did not wish to regard any semantic relations connecting words and sentences with things and states of affairs as part of the ideal scientific conceptual scheme. But, again like Williams, Sellars wished to say that our ordinary-language schemes somehow reflect (are perspectives on) the objective world. So Sellars introduced a relation he called "picturing", to be distinguished from truth and reference, and said that our ordinary-language schemes (our local perspectives) "picture" the world more or less adequately (some of our schemes more adequately and some less), even if they do not bear an objective semantic relation to it. The difficulty, which has split Sellars' students and followers into two camps,[29] is that Sellars owes us at least a sketch of how picturing can be defined in the ideal scientific scheme. Where Williams differs from Sellars is apparently in not recognizing the problem. Yet without giving sense to the notion that the marks and noises which constitute our various "perspectives", and also the marks and noises which constitute the absolute conception of the world, somehow *picture* the world, Williams cannot sustain the idea that these marks and noises *are*, respectively, our local perspectives and an objective description. To be a "perspective", marks and noises must *picture* something; to be an objective description, marks and noises must *describe*.

I was, perhaps, unfair to accuse Williams of not seeing the problem at all. It is, very likely, because he faces this problem that he replaces talk of the absolute conception's "explaining the possibility" of the local conceptions with talk of our being able to explain the local conceptions with its aid. Thus, in one passage,[30] Williams says of the absolute conception, "it will also help to explain to us, *though not necessarily to those alien investigators*, such things as our capacity to grasp that conception" (emphasis added). In other words, the "theory of error" will not be provided by the absolute conception, but will be part of a "local perspective", albeit one that is informed by the absolute conception (Williams repeatedly mentions neurobiology). But such a theory will be a theory whose central notion, the notion of picturing or describing the world (perspectivally or non-perspectivally) does not belong to the absolute conception. Is Williams saying that it is just our local perspective that there *is* an absolute conception? Even Richard Rorty might agree with that.

The third feature of the absolute conception is that the convergence of all species of researchers (ourselves and alien species) on the absolute conception of the world will, if it comes about, be explained by the fact that that is "how things (anyway) are", or how things are independent of experience. This presupposes both the notion of convergence, that is to say, agreement in belief, and the notion that, given a belief, one can say that what the belief *says* (not the marks and noises used to express the belief) "is how things are"—that is, the notion that a belief describes (or at least "pictures") something outside itself. But Williams takes seriously the Quinian idea of the indeterminacy of reference: "If the various sorts of considerations which have been summarily sketched here are correct, then we have to give up not just dualism but the belief in the determinacy of the mental. These considerations converge on the conclusion that there are no fully determinate contents of the world which are its psychological contents" (*Descartes*, p. 300).

Williams might, of course, have chosen to regard the notion of the "content" of a belief as one which *will* be available in the absolute conception of the world. But in that case he would have had either to show that that notion can be reduced to the notions of physics, which he is persuaded by Quine and Davidson is not a promising line to take, or to follow Fodor in trying to reduce it to notions from the special sciences and/or the ordinary-language "thick" notion of causation (which, I believe, he would regard as too "local"), or to take it as primitive. If he had followed the last course, he would have had to admit that we do *not* have a sketch of the "absolute conception of the world" in present-day physics; that, indeed, the notion of an absolute conception of the world is either just the ordinary notion of an objective description or a we-know-not-what. In either case, his insistence that normative notions cannot appear in the absolute conception becomes groundless; for that insistence was based from beginning to end on the idea that only primary qualities can appear in the absolute conception.

Indeed, it is precisely because Williams refuses to admit normative notions into the absolute conception that the indeterminacy of translation appears to be such a threat. For an indeterminacy of translation that affects only the interpretation of subsentential parts, however perplexing, and whatever we may decide about it, will not prevent us from seeing our sentences as related to an objective world as long as sentences as wholes have determinate conditions of warranted assertability. It is striking that when Williams describes the indeterminacy he is talking about, he describes it by saying that a sentence may have two correct translations which are not themselves "equivalent".[31]

It is, of course, true that this can happen in cases of ordinary vagueness or ambiguity. If S itself is ambiguous, and A and B are the alternative ways of disambiguating it, then it is not surprising that A and B may be equally plausible but non-equivalent translations, and if the speaker was unclear as to what he or she meant to convey, A and B may be equally correct. But no one would call this an example of the "indeterminacy of translation" in Quine's sense. The kind of indeterminacy Williams refers to is a serious threat only if *there is no fact of the matter as to what the conditions of warranted assertibility of even an unambiguous sentence are.*[32] But to believe this is to believe that there is no fact of the matter about the normative—and not just about that small part of the normative which we call the ethical.

If Williams were to drop his endorsement of the indeterminacy thesis, and to admit that we can make no sense of an adequate conception of the world (whether we call it "absolute" or not) that does not make room for normative notions, I would regard the position as greatly improved. But I would still urge him to recognize that there are many true descriptions of the world in many different vocabularies, without trying to privilege one of those descriptions as the "absolute" one. This idea will play a central role when I come to examine Nelson Goodman's position.

The "Truth in Relativism"

Williams' discovery of a "truth in relativism" does not appear to me to be any more coherent than the "absolute conception of the world". First, let me point out something that I have not had occasion to remark up to now: Williams is extremely cavalier about the notion of truth. Sometimes the truth is what is "tracked" by the practices of a linguistic community; but at other times Williams treats truth simply "disquotationally", that is, he applies the principle that if *we* assert S then *we* must say that S is true, without invoking any considerations of "tracking".

This is, for example, the way Williams treats the use of the word "true" in what he calls "real confrontations". It is striking that the same cavalier attitude is characteristic of a philosopher Williams regards as an opponent—Richard Rorty. Like Williams, Rorty sometimes treats truth as right assertibility in a local language game, and sometimes treats it disquotationally, or as a "compliment" we pay to opinions we like. Moreover, again like Williams, Rorty is fond of insisting that we are related to the world *causally* but not *semantically*.[33] It is true that Rorty rejects the idea of an "absolute conception of the world"—but if it were made clear to Rorty that the conception in question is "absolute" *only from our local perspective*, would he still feel it necessary to reject it? Could it be that, even if they do not recognize it, Rorty and Williams are in complete agreement in metaphysics? For the rest, I shall content myself with two observations.

(1) The distinction between "real" and "notional" confrontations is unfortunately drawn, even for Williams' own purposes. As it stands, the confrontation between the Jews and the Nazis would not count as a real confrontation by Williams' definition—because "going over to" the point of view of the other was not a "real option" for either the Jews or the Nazis. Yet Williams would not deny that it is appropriate to use the language of good and bad, right and wrong, in such a conflict. How Williams' distinction might be repaired to remove this inconsistency is something I shall not speculate about.

(2) Williams says that in a notional conflict "the question of truth does not genuinely arise". Yet he also says that the members of the other community, the one from which I am relatively distant, have ethical *knowledge*,[34] and that their beliefs (when they deploy their concepts carefully) are true.[35] This is a blatant contradiction, and I do not see how to remove it.[36] For example, it will not do to to reply as follows:[37] when I want to talk about

one of the concepts of the distant community, and to reject the values embedded in its thick concepts, I can say "I agree that doing such-and-such is unchaste, but I don't regard chastity as a virtue" (that is, conflict is registered using the "thin" concepts such as *good, right* or *virtue;* this would still allow us to say that the distant community's thick judgements are true). First of all, there are many things that traditional communities regard as unchaste (such as, in traditional Muslim communities, women appearing in public without veils, or, in ultra-Orthodox Jewish communities, a woman being alone with a man in a room with a closed door, if the man is not her husband or father)[38] which we do not regard as unchaste. We would not say "we agree that her being alone in the office with her employer is unchaste but we don't think chastity is a virtue", for even those of us who do think chastity is a virtue don't regard *that* as unchaste. Second, this reply would contradict Williams' explicit statement[39] that only in the case of real conflict can the language of appraisal (including "true" and "false") be used. It is a flat-out contradiction to say that the judgment that the act is unchaste is true (although we are "disbarred" from making it) and also to say that we can't say that the judgment is either true or false.

Metaphysics and Entanglement

What led Williams to defend this complicated metaphysical theory was the desire to assert a "truth in relativism" while resisting relativism in science. But in the process of building up this intricate construction with its two kinds of truth (ordinary and "absolute"), its perspectivalism about secondary qualities and ethics (and, oddly, also about the intentional) and its anti-perspectivalism about physics, he often ignores the entanglement of the factual and the ethical—although he himself stresses that entanglement at other points in his discussion. Consider, for example, the question as to whether we can condemn the Aztec way of life, or, more specifically, the human sacrifice that the Aztecs engaged in. On Williams' view, the Aztec belief that there were supernatural beings who would be angry with the Aztecs if they did not perform the sacrifices was, as a matter of scientific fact, wrong. This belief we *can* evaluate. It is simply false; and the absolute conception of the world, to the extent we can now approximate it, tells us that it is false. But we cannot say that the Aztec way of life was wrong. Yet the feature of the Aztecs' way of life that troubles us (the human sacrifice) and their belief about the world that conflicts with science were interdependent. If we can say that the Aztec belief about the gods was false, why can we not say that the practice to which it led was wrong (although, to be sure, understandable given the false factual belief)? If we are not allowed to call the practice wrong, why are we allowed to call the belief false? The so-called "absolute" and the ethical are just as entangled as the "factual" and the ethical.

For a very different sort of example, consider the admiration we sometimes feel for the Amish (traditional Mennonite) way of life. Even atheists sometimes admire the community solidarity, the helpfulness, and the simplicity of the Amish way. If sophisticated atheists who felt this way were asked why they admire the Amish, they might reply something like this: "I am not necessarily saying we should give up our individualism altogether. But the kind of individualism and competitiveness which has brought so much scientific and economic progress also brings with it egotism, arrogance, selfishness, and downright cruelty. Even if the Amish way of life rests on what I regard as false beliefs, it does show some of the possibilities of a less competitive, less individualistic form of life; and perhaps we can learn about these possibilities from the Amish without adopting their religion." Now, Williams does not deny that we can say things like this—that we can learn from cultures to which we stand in the relation he calls "the relativity of distance", cultures which are not "real options" for us. But how does this differ from saying "some of the Amish beliefs are false, but other of their beliefs may be true"? Williams' examples load the dice in favor of relativism by taking science to consist of individual judgments which may be called true or false, while taking "cultures" to offer only "take it as a whole or reject it as a whole" options.[40]

The problem with the whole enterprise lies right here: Williams wants to acknowledge the entanglement of fact and value and hold on to the "absolute" character of (ideal) scientific knowledge at the same time. But there is no way to do this. It cannot be the case that scientific knowledge (future fundamental physics) is absolute and nothing else is; for fundamental physics cannot explain the possibility of *referring to* or *stating* anything, including fundamental physics itself. So, if everything that is *not* physics is "perspectival", then the notion of the "absolute" is itself hopelessly perspectival. And the idea of a "relativism of distance" which applies to ethics but not to science also fails, because ethics and science are as entangled as ethics and "fact". What we have in *Ethics and the Limits of Philosophy* is, in fact, not a serious argument for ethical "non-objectivism", but rather the expression of a mood. In *Ethics and the Limits of Philosophy*, we are told that ethical "non-objectivism" is the "contemporary" point of view, and what is being offered is a *sophisticated reflection on the consequences of this presupposition*. The sophistication is undeniable, and many wonderful observations and arguments occur in the course of the reflection. But the presupposition itself does not stand up to any kind of examination—or at least, the ways in which Williams defends the presupposition crumble when one subjects them to careful examination.

6

Irrealism and Deconstruction

As we saw in the last chapter, Bernard Williams, who views physics as giving us the ultimate metaphysical truth, thinks that ethical statements and normative statements generally have truth values which presuppose the perspective of "some social world or other". Outright relativists about truth would agree with this conclusion, though not with Bernard Williams' metaphysics. As we have seen, however, neither physicalism nor relativism has been successful. Attempts to define reference in terms of "causal attachment" have failed, and relativist attempts to define truth, which I discussed in Chapter 4, lead to a tangle of self-contradictory or solipsistic or otherwise unacceptable consequences. Bernard Williams' move, which is to say that talk of the "content" of a belief (that is, talk of its reference and truth) is itself "perspectival", lacks any clear sense. This state of affairs has been grist for the mills of deconstruction. Deconstructionists think that the whole idea of representing reality, indeed the whole idea of "reality", needs to be deconstructed. The tangles in which scientific realists and relativists involve themselves are only manifestation of the incoherence of the very idea of truth. Indeed, Rorty himself, as I have mentioned, has moved from a relativist to a deconstructionist position (Rorty cites the father of deconstruction, Jacques Derrida, as one of his heroes).[1] Unlike Rorty, however, Derrida has never suggested that we should try to get along without the notion of truth; the notion may be incoherent, but we have no way of doing without it, according to Derrida.

In the opinion of most analytic philosophers, trying to criticize deconstruction is like trying to have a fistfight with a fog. Indeed, although Derrida does not disdain argument, some of his followers seem to scorn it. The very habit of arguing in a close analytic fashion is seen by many deconstructionists as a sign that one is "out of it".

But there *are* arguments to be found in Derrida's writing, although they are usually alluded to rather than actually given. Although Derrida complains about the "assertoric style" in philosophy, his own writing tends to consist of one assertion after another. I shall discuss some of those arguments a little later. But first I want to discuss the views of a philosopher who does delight in argument, an American analytic philosopher, not a French deconstructionist, who has reached conclusions in some ways perilously close to Derrida's: Nelson Goodman.

Nelson Goodman's "Irrealism"

Goodman first announced his "irrealism" in a challenging and unquestionably path-breaking little book provocatively titled *Ways of Worldmaking*. The title captures two of the most important claims of the book: that we inhabit not one world, but many simultaneously; and that these worlds are worlds of our own making.

The idea of a plurality of worlds is connected with an idea I shall look at shortly, the idea that there is not one unique "right version" of the world, but rather a number of different "right versions" of it. This is an idea that I agree with. An example— mine, not Goodman's—is that there is no unique right version of the relation between ordinary objects (tables and trees and animals) and scientific objects. We can speak as if such ordinary objects were identical with scientific objects, or as if they were distinct from the physical systems which constitute their matter,[2] or we can say that which physical system a given common sense object is identical with is to some degree vague (as I would urge) but that there are some physical systems that this chair, or whatever the example may be, is definitely *not* identical with. Moreover, there are many possible choices as to what we should take the physical system to be, if we want to identify chairs and trees with physical systems: space-time regions (or the gravitational, electromagnetic, and other fields that occupy those regions), or aggregates of portions of the histories of various molecules. Each of these ways of speaking can be formalized, and each of the resulting formalisms[3] represents a perfectly admissible way of speaking; but Goodman would say (and I would agree) none of them can claim to be "the way things are independent of experience". There is no one uniquely true description of reality.

The idea that the facts admit of more than one picture has been around for over a century, however. It is anticipated by Herz's talk of equally good "world pictures" in the introduction to his *Principles of Mechanics*, and it is referred to by William James.[4] Goodman's innovation is to attack the claim that our conceptual schemes *are* just different "descriptions" of what are in some sense "the same facts". Goodman regards this idea as empty. For him it is immaterial whether we speak of versions as descriptions of worlds or say that there are no worlds and only versions. What Goodman is adamant about, however, is that if we do choose to speak of worlds as distinct from versions, then we must say that incompatible versions refer to different worlds. It cannot be true of one and the same world that the space-time points are individual things and that they are abstractions. Thus we ought to say—if we keep the concept of a world at all—not that we describe the world (as philosophers) sometimes using a language in which tables and chairs are talked of as aggregates of "time-slices" of molecules and sometimes using a language in which those aggregates of "time-slices" of molecules are regarded as the *matter* of the tables and chairs (and the matter is spoken of as something distinct from the table or chair); but rather that we *sometimes choose to make a world in which tables and chair are aggregates of "time-slices" of molecules and sometimes choose to make a world in which tables and chairs are distinct from those aggregates of "time-slices" of molecules.* Goodman confronts us with a choice between saying that there are many worlds or that world-talk is nonsense.[5] True to his own pluralism, Goodman sometimes speaks as if there were no world(s) at all, and sometimes speaks as if there were many.

But if we choose to speak of worlds, where do these worlds come from? Goodman's answer is unequivocal: they are made by us. They are not made *ex nihilo*, but out of previous worlds— or out of previous versions, since the distinction between a world and a version is of no moment. Springing full-blown within contemporary analytic philosophy, a form of idealism as extreme as Hegel's or Fichte's!

In addition to Goodman's more technical arguments, there is a more accessible argument that he first used in commenting on the papers in a symposium on *Ways of Worldmaking* at the December meeting of the American Philosophical Association in 1979.[6] Goodman discussed the question, raised by Israel Scheffler, "Is it a consequence of Goodman's philosophy that *we made the stars?*" Goodman answered that while there is a sense in which we did not make the stars (we don't make stars in the way in which a brickmaker makes a brick), there is indeed a sense in which we did make the stars. Goodman illustrated this by asking us to consider a constellation, say the Big Dipper. Did we make the Big Dipper? There is an obvious sense in which the answer is no. All right, we didn't make it in the way in which a carpenter makes a table, but *did we make it a constellation?* Did we make it the Big Dipper? At this point, perhaps many of us might say yes, there is a sense in which we made "it" the Big Dipper. After all, it is hard to think of the fact that a group of stars is a "dipper" as one which is mind independent or language independent. Perhaps we should give Goodman this much, that we didn't "make" the Big Dipper as a carpenter makes a table, but we did make it by constructing a version in which that group of stars is seen as exhibiting a dipper shape, and by giving it a name, thus, as it were, institutionalizing the fact that that group of stars is metaphorically a big dipper. Nowadays, there is a Big Dipper up there in the sky, and we, so to speak, "put" a Big Dipper up there in the sky by constructing that version. But—and Goodman is, of course, waiting for this objection—we didn't make the stars of which that constellation consists. Stars are a "natural kind", whereas constellations are an "artificial kind".[7]

But let us take a look at this so-called natural kind. Natural kinds, when we examine them, almost always turn out to have boundaries which are to some degree arbitrary, even if the degree of arbitrariness is much less than in the case of a completely conventional kind like "constellation".[8] Stars are clouds of glowing gas, glowing because of thermonuclear reactions which are caused by the gravitational field of the star itself, but not every cloud of glowing gas is considered a star; some such clouds fall into other astronomical categories, and some stars do not glow at all. Is it not *we* who group together all these different objects into a single category "star" with our inclusions and exclusions? It is true that we did not make the stars as a carpenter makes a table, but didn't we, after all, *make them stars?*

Now Goodman makes a daring extrapolation. He proposes that in the sense illustrated by these examples, the sense in which we "make" certain things the Big Dipper and make certain things stars, there is nothing that we did not make to be what it is. (Theologically, one might say that Goodman makes man the Creator.) If, for example, you say that we didn't make the elementary particles, Goodman can point to the present situation in quantum mechanics and ask whether you really want to view elementary particles as a mind-independent reality.[9] It is clear that if we try to beat Goodman at his own game, by trying to name some "mind-independent stuff", we shall be in deep trouble.

In spite of its elegance, it seems to me that this little argument of Goodman's is easily defused. There *is* a fundamental difference between the terms "constellation" and "Big Dipper", on the one hand, and a term like "star" on the other. The extension of the term "Big Dipper" is fixed by linguistic convention. The term applies to a finite group of stars, and one learns which stars are in the group and how they are arranged when one learns the meaning of the term. In this respect, "Big Dipper" is a typical *proper name*.

We know which stars belong to the Big Dipper by knowing what it is we call "the Big Dipper". I would not say that it is "analytic" that the Big Dipper contains *all* of those stars, because if one of those stars "went out" or was totally removed by aliens with vast superscientific powers we would undoubtedly go on speaking of the Big Dipper and just say that the Big Dipper didn't have as many stars as it used to have. In the same way, we will continue to refer to John Smith as "John Smith" even if he loses his hair. (If a new star appeared "in" the Big Dipper, however, it would not automatically count as a part of the Big Dipper. Whether it came to count as a part of the Big Dipper would depend entirely on subsequent linguistic practice; which stars are part of the Big Dipper is a question for an anthropologist or a linguist, not a question for an astrophysicist.)

In contrast to the term "Big Dipper", the term "star" has an extension that cannot be fixed by giving a list. And no particular object is in the extension of "star" simply by virtue of being *called* a star; it might be crazy to doubt that Sirius is really a star, but someone who thought that Sirius is really a giant light bulb or a glowing spaceship wouldn't thereby show an inability to use "star" in the way in which someone who doubted that that constellation is really the Big Dipper would show an inability to use "Big Dipper".

In these respects, the term "constellation" lies somewhere in between "Big Dipper" and "star". If we discovered that all the stars in the Big Dipper are really giant fakes installed to fool us by those superscientific aliens (giant light bulbs in the sky, so to speak), we would say "they aren't really stars", but we wouldn't say "that isn't really the Big Dipper". Would we cease to regard the Big Dipper as a constellation? Perhaps we would, but I am completely unsure.

The upshot is very simple. One perfectly good answer to Goodman's rhetorical question "Can you tell me something that we didn't make?" is that we didn't make Sirius a star. Not only didn't we make Sirius a star in the sense in which a carpenter makes a table, *we didn't make it a star*. Our ancestors and our contemporaries (including astrophysicists), in shaping and creating our language, created the concept *star*, with its partly conventional boundaries, with its partly indeterminate boundaries, and so on. And that concept *applies to* Sirius. The fact that the concept *star* has conventional elements doesn't mean that *we* make it the case that that concept applies to any particular thing, in the way in which we made it the case that the concept "Big Dipper" applies to a particular group of stars.

The concept *bachelor* is far more strongly conventional than the concept *star*, and that concept applies to Joseph Ullian, but our linguistic practices didn't make Joe a bachelor. (They did make him "Joe Ullian".)[10] General names like "star" and "bachelor" are very different from proper names like "the Big Dipper" and "Joe Ullian", and Goodman's argument depends upon our not noticing the difference.

Irrealism and Conceptual Relativity

Goodman has far more serious arguments for his theses, and these arguments contain many real insights (even if they lead to wrong conclusions). We have to discuss them with some delicacy. Those arguments depend on a phenomenon I have called "conceptual relativity".[11] Here is an example. Points in space (or nowadays one often refers instead to points in space-time) can be regarded as concrete[12] particulars of which space consists (the ultimate parts of space) or, alternatively, as "mere limits".[13] Geometrical discourse can be adequately formalized from either point of view;[14] so can all of physics. And whether formalized or left unformalized, both ways of speaking will do perfectly well for all the purposes of geometry and physics.

Goodman regards these two versions of space-time theory as "incompatible". At the same time, he regards them as both right. And since incompatible versions cannot be true of the same world, he concludes that they are true of different worlds "if true of any".

One well-known objection to views like Goodman's has been advanced by Donald Davidson[15] (and Quine has recently been converted to it as well). Davidson's argument is as quick and dirty as Goodman's: Davidson simply accepts Goodman's view that the two versions are incompatible, points out that according to standard logic incompatible statements cannot both be true, and concludes that it is unintelligible to maintain that both versions are true. Even if both versions are equally good for practical purposes, I cannot say that they are both true, according to Davidson and Quine. Quine does say[16] that I may pick one of these versions some of the time (say Mondays, Wednesdays, and Fridays?) and the other one at other times, but at any given time I must say that the version I am using then is true and the version I am not using then is false, on pain of self-contradiction.

Goodman's view, as we have seen, is to say that logic does indeed tell us that incompatible statements cannot both be true *of the same world*, but, in his view, the equal "rightness" of both of these incompatible versions shows that they are true *of different worlds*. Davidson does not explicitly discuss this move, but Quine rejects it on the ground that to split reality into a number of different worlds is to violate the principle of parsimony. (The possibility of saying that there are no worlds at all, that is, no extralinguistic reality, is one that Quine apparently does not deem worthy of discussion.)

Goodman and Davidson seem to me to be making the same mistake—although, as often happens in philosophy, it leads them into opposite camps. Davidson and Goodman both accept without question the idea that statements which appear to be incompatible, taken according to their surface grammar, really are incompatible, even in cases like these. If the sentence, "points are mere limits" is a contrary of the sentence "points are not limits but parts of space", even when the first sentence occurs in a systematic scheme for describing physical reality and the second occurs in another systematic scheme for describing physical reality *even though the two schemes are in practice thoroughly equivalent*,[17] then we are in trouble indeed. But the whole point of saying that the two schemes are in practice thoroughly equivalent is that, far from leading us to incompatible predictions or incompatible actions, it makes no difference to our predictions or actions which of the two schemes we use. Nor are the two schemes "equivalent" only in the weak sense of what is sometimes called "empirical equivalence" (that is, leading to the same predictions); rather, each sentence in one of them, say the scheme in which points are concrete particulars, can be correlated in an effective way with a "translation" in the other scheme, and the sentence and its translation will be used to describe the same states of affairs.

In saying that they are used to describe the same states of affairs, I am not introducing a transcendent ontology of states of affairs. By a "state of affairs" I mean something like a particle's being at a point, or a place X's being between a place Y and a place Z; in short, I assume a familiar language to be already in place. I am not saying that Noumenal Reality consists of states of affairs. (I could have spoken of "situations", or "physical events", or in many other ways. The relation of language to the world is also something that can be described in more than one way.) Nor am I assuming a one-to-one correspondence between sentences and states of affairs, thus populating the world with "sentence-shaped objects", in a phrase taken from Richard Rorty. The whole point of what I just said is that very *different* sentences can describe the very same state of affairs. In short, what I meant by a "state of affairs" when I said that a sentence in one formalization of physical geometry and its "translation" in the alternative formalization will be used to describe the same "states of affairs" is just what anyone would mean by that phrase who was *not* giving it a metaphysical emphasis.

That the sentences in one such scheme that we use in practice can be correlated with the sentences in another such scheme was pointed out long ago by Goodman himself. The nature of such correlations was studied by Goodman,[18] who referred to this kind of correlation as "extensional isomorphism". Am I am saying, then, that the sentence "points are mere limits" and the sentence "points are not mere limits but parts of space" actually have the same meaning? Not at all. Some sentences function virtually as tautologies within their own "version". If we identify points with limits by definition, then, in our version, "points are mere limits" will be a conventional truth. And we do not generally translate such conventional truths in one version into the other version (although we could; we could, for example, translate every quasi-logical truth in the one version by any fixed tautology in the other). But the more interesting, less conventional, truths in the one version— say, theorems of ordinary Euclidean geometry, or the statement that there is a particle with a certain mass at a certain place— can be "translated" from one version into another version; these are the statements for which we provide correlates.

Should we say that any such statement in the version in which points are treated as concrete particulars—say, the statement that between any two points on a line there is a third point—has exactly the same *meaning* as its "translation" into the version in which points are identified with limits (say, with convergent sets of concentric spheres)? I would say that in the context of real-life physics and real-life mathematics it makes no difference which of these two ways one talks and thinks. I am saying that if a sentence in one version is true in that version, then its correlate in the other version is true in the other version. But to ask if these two sentences have the same meaning is to try to force the ordinary-language notion of meaning to do a job for which it was never designed.

The phenomenon of conceptual relativity is a mind-boggling one. To suppose that questions like "Do S_1 and S_2 have the same meaning or a different meaning?" make any sense in *this* case seems to me precisely the assumption that we should not make. The sentence "Between any two points on a line there is a third point" and its "translation" into the version in which points are identified with convergent sets of concentric spheres have the same truth conditions in the sense that they are mathematically equivalent. The answer to the question "Do the two sentences have the same meaning?" is that the ordinary notion of meaning simply crumbles in the face of such a question. It was never meant to do *that* job.[19]

Now to the question of "incompatibility", which exercises both Goodman and Davidson so: "point", "line", "limit", and so on are used in different ways in the two versions. To say that the sentence "points are convergent sets of concentric spheres",[20] as used in the one version, is incompatible with "points are not sets but individuals", as used in the other version, is much too simple. Rather than conclude with Goodman that either there is no world at all or else we live in more than one world, or to conclude with Davidson that the phenomenon of equivalent descriptions, which we have recognized in science since the end of the nineteenth century, somehow involves a logical contradiction, we should simply give up the idea that the sentences we have been discussing preserve something called their "meaning" when we go from one such version into another such version.

Am I not, then, saying that the sentence has a *different* meaning in the two versions? (If a sentence doesn't preserve its meaning, it must change it, right?) I repeat that the answer is that the notion of "meaning", and the ordinary practices of translation and paraphrase to which it is linked, crumble when confronted with such cases. We can say that the words "point", "limit", and so forth have different "uses" in these two versions, if we like. In view of that difference in use, one should not treat a sentence in one version as though it contradicted what the same physicists or the same mathematicians might say on another day when they are employing the other version. But whether such a change of use is or is not a change of "meaning" is not a question that need have an answer.

The Significance of Conceptual Relativity

The significance of conceptual relativity might come out more clearly if we consider a somewhat different case. In *The Many Faces of Realism* I described in detail a case in which the same situation, in a perfectly commonsensical sense of "the same situation", can be described as involving entirely different numbers and kinds of objects (colored "atoms" alone, versus colored atoms plus "aggregates" of atoms). If you have a world in which there are two black "atoms" and one red one you can either say that there are three objects (the atoms), or that there are seven objects (the atoms and the various aggregates of two or more atoms). How many objects are there "really" in such a world? I suggest that *either way of describing it is equally "true"*. The idea that "object" has some sense which is independent of how we are counting objects and what we are counting as an "object" in a given situation is an illusion. I do not mean by this that there "really" are "aggregates", and there really are atoms and there really are sets and there really are numbers, and so on, and it is just that *sometimes* "object" does not refer to "all objects". I mean that the metaphysical notion of "all objects" has no sense.

Again, in quantum mechanics, any two states of a system can be in a "superposition"; that is to say, any particular state of a system, involving having a particular number of particles or a particular energy or a particular momentum, can be represented by a kind of "vector" in an abstract space, and the superposition of any two such states can be represented by forming a vector sum. These vector sums are sometimes classically very difficult to interpret: what do we make of a state in which the answer to the question "How many electrons are there in this box?" is "Well, there is a superposition of there being three electrons in the box and there being seventeen"? But we can represent such unthinkable states mathematically, and we know how to derive predictions and formulate explanations using them. This principle of superposition applies to field theory as well as to particle theory; the "field states" of the quantum field theorist are not the field states of the classical field theorist; they are typically *superpositions* of the field states of the classical theory. We may say, then (and here I leave out entirely the puzzling role of the observer in quantum mechanics), that from the point of view of quantum mechanics, the world consists of fields in "funny" states. But—and this was the discovery of Richard Feynman—it is also possible to think in a very different way. We can think of the world as consisting of particles (although we have to vastly increase the number of particles we postulate in order to carry this through) and we can think of any situation that we describe in field physics as a superposition of an infinite number of different *particle* situations. In short, there are two different ways of thinking in quantum field theory. In one way of thinking, the way the physicist thinks when performing the usual field calculations, the system is in a superposition of field states. In the other way of thinking, the way of thinking when drawing "Feynman diagrams", the system is in a superposition of particle states. In short, the system may be thought of as consisting either of fields or of particles, but it cannot be thought of as consisting of either classical fields or classical particles.

Consider a given physical system which the physicist represents twice over, once in the language of fields and once in the language of particles (say, by drawing Feynman diagrams). What I am saying is that this is a real system, and that these are two legitimate ways of talking about that real system. The fact that the real system allows itself to be talked about in these two very different ways does not mean either that there is no real physical system being talked about, or that there are two different physical systems in two different Goodmanian worlds being talked about.

The point is even clearer in the case of the first example, the example in which "the same situation" was described as involving entirely different numbers and kinds of objects. It is absolutely clear, it seems to me, that the two descriptions are descriptions of *one and the same world*, not two different worlds.

Part of Goodman's challenge—as it was part of the challenge of German idealists like Hegel and Fichte in the beginning of the nineteenth century—is to say, "Well, if you say that these two ways of talking are both descriptions of the same reality, then *describe that reality as it is apart from those ways of talking*." But why should one suppose that reality can be described independent of our descriptions? And why should the fact that reality cannot be described independent of our descriptions lead us to suppose that there are only the descriptions? After all, according to our descriptions themselves, the word "quark" is one thing and a quark is quite a different thing.

Nevertheless, the phenomenon of conceptual relativity does have real philosophical importance. As long as we think of the world as consisting of objects and properties in some one, philosophically preferred sense of "object" and "property"—as long as we think that reality itself, if viewed with enough metaphysical seriousness, will *determine* for us how we are to use the words "object" and "property"—then we will not see how the number and kind of objects and their properties can vary from one correct description of a situation[21] to another correct description of that same situation. Although our sentences do "correspond to reality" in the sense of describing it, they are not simply copies of reality. To revert for a second to Bernard Williams' book, the idea that some descriptions are "descriptions of reality as it is independent of perspective" is a chimera. Our language cannot be divided up into two parts, a part that describes the world "as it is anyway" and a part that describes our conceptual contribution. This does not mean that reality is hidden or noumenal; it simply means that you can't describe the world without describing it.

Irrealism and Deconstruction

We may now begin to appraise the frequently heard claim that "the problematique of representation has collapsed".[22] What people who talk like this mean is that the notion of reference to an objective world has collapsed. Goodman's work has the virtue of setting forth an *argument* for this position which is much clearer than any that one can extract from the work of Derrida. Goodman's argument does, I have claimed, destroy one traditional version of "realism", the version I like to call metaphysical realism.[23] According to that version, the notions of an object and a property each have just one philosophically serious "meaning", and the world divides itself up into objects and properties in one definite unique way. This is the myth of the ready-made world. (This is also one form of what Derrida would call the "metaphysics of presence".)

The myth of the ready-made world is a myth which has become linked with a number of other ideas. For example, there is the expectation, which we have already encountered, that the objects and properties of which the world ("in itself") consists are the objects and properties of "finished science", and there is the tendency—it is much more than a tendency in fact—to forget that the principle of bivalence of classical logic is simply a useful idealization, which is not conformed to fully and cannot be conformed to fully by any actual language, natural or artificial, that human beings could possibly use.

But the collapse of a certain picture of the world, and of the conceptions of representation and truth that went with that picture of the world, is very far from being a collapse of the notions of representation and truth. To identify the collapse of one philosophical picture of representation with the collapse of the idea that we represent things that we did not bring into existence is, quite simply, dotty. Deconstructionists are right in claiming that a certain philosophical tradition is bankrupt; but to identify that metaphysical tradition with our lives and our language is to give metaphysics an altogether exaggerated importance. For deconstructionists, metaphysics was the *basis* of our entire culture, the pedestal on which it all rested; if the pedestal has broken, the entire culture must have collapsed— indeed, our whole language must lie in ruins. But of course we can and do make sense of the idea of a reality we did not make, even though we cannot make sense of the idea of a reality that is "present" in the metaphysical sense of dictating its own unique description. As we saw, seemingly incompatible words may actually describe the same situation or event or the same physical system.

At this point we run into another source of contemporary philosophical scepticism. This source is the doctrine of incommensurability. Although that doctrine has been associated in recent years with the writings of Thomas Kuhn, it appeared in French thought decades before Kuhn's work. A version of it appeared in Ferdinand Saussure's *Cours de linquistique generale*,[24] a work whose influence on both structuralist and poststructuralist French philosophy is unquestionable. Saussure's route to incommensurability was the following: along with other linguists of his time (for example, the Prague school) Saussure

learned that the basic phonetic units of language, the phonemes, were not themselves identifiable in terms of their physical features. One can characterize a phoneme in a language
only by contrast with the other phonemes in the language. It
is the whole system of contrasts that determines what the phonemes of a given language are. Phonemes are not "sounds" in
the physicist's sense of sound. One cannot say that the English
phoneme p is the "same" as the German phoneme p; they
simply belong to different systems of contrasts. Saussure assumed that something similar would have to be true of the
semantic units of the language; that is, he assumed that the
meanings expressible in a language could be characterized only
by the ways in which they contrasted or failed to contrast with
other meanings available in the same language. The idea of
describing the language as a system of differences (a system of
available contrasts) was to be extended from phonemics to semantics.

But different languages do not, in fact, provide the same
semantical contrasts. A language which recognizes only four
fundamental colors provides a different system of contrasts from
one which provides seven fundamental colors, for example.
The line of thinking that Saussure had embarked on leads fairly
quickly to the conclusion that meanings are parochial to languages (and from here it is not far to the thought that they may
be parochial to individual "texts"). No two languages ever express the same meanings; no meaning can ever be expressed in
more than one language (or even text). The very notion of a
sign's meaning, as something separable from the sign, collapses.

In an interview with Kristeva,[25] Derrida makes clear his
wholehearted acceptance of this line of thinking; he criticizes
Saussure only for not going further and abandoning talk of
"signs" altogether (since the notion of a "signified" independent
of the system of signs has collapsed):

To take only one example, one could show that a semiology of the Saussurean type has had a double role. *On the one hand*, an absolutely decisive role:

1. It has marked, against the tradition, that the signified is inseparable from the signifier, that the signified and the signifier are two sides of one and the same coin. Saussure even purposefully refused to have this opposition or this "two-sided unity" conform to the relationship between soul and body, as had always been done. "This two-sided unity has often been compared to the unity of the human person, composed of a body and a soul. The comparison is hardly satisfactory."[26]

2. By emphasizing the *differential* and *formal* characteristics of semiological functioning, by showing that it is "impossible for sound, the material element, itself to belong to language", and that "in its essence it [the linguistic signifier] is not at all phonic";[27] by desubstantializing both the signified content and the "expressive substance"—which therefore is no longer in a privileged or exclusive way phonic—by making linguistics a division of general semiology—Saussure powerfully contributed to turning against the metaphysical tradition the concept of the sign that he borrowed from it.

Derrida fails to notice that a Utopian project lay behind Saussure's way of thinking. The hope was for a strictly scientific account of meaning, one that would exactly parallel the structure of the newly emergent phonemics. Since that hope has collapsed (it was hardly coherent to begin with), we are not forced to the bizarre view that no one can understand any language but his or her own ideolect. Nor does Derrida himself go so far; like Quine, after having denounced the notion of meaning-preserving translation, he recognizes the indispensability of translation in practice, although in a very guarded way:

> In the limits to which it is possible, or at least *appears* possible, translation practices the difference between signified and signifier.[28] But if this difference is never pure, no more

so is translation, and for the notion of translation we would have to substitute the notion of *transformation:* a regulated transformation of one language by another, of one text by another. We will never have, and in fact never had, to do with some "transport" of pure signifieds from one language to another, or within one and the same language, that the signifying instrument would leave virgin and untouched. (*Positions*, p. 20; emphasis in the original)

The alternative to Saussure's view is to keep the notion of "sameness of meaning" while recognizing that it is not to be interpreted as the self-identity of objects called "meanings" or "signifieds". When two uses of words may be regarded as "the same" and when they may be regarded as "not the same" is not a matter of some clean mathematical relation of equivalence or non-equivalence between two systems of contrasts. If people inquire about the meaning of something that someone says, we generally have some idea as to why they are asking and what they are going to do with the answer. Given the context and the interests of the people involved, we can usually come up with a pretty good answer. Can it be that in Derrida's use of Saussure we see some of the same mistakes that are made by American analytic philosophers like Jerry Fodor? Fodor would, of course, reject the idea, which is implicit in the argument I have cited, that sameness of meaning makes strict sense only in the impossible case in which the two languages or texts in question are *isomorphic.* But the fact that Derrida takes this idea seriously, while not even considering the possibility that the kind of "sameness of meaning" we seek in translation might be an interest-relative (but still quite real) relation, one which involves a normative judgment, a judgment as to what is *reasonable* in the particular case, does remind me of Fodor's scientism.

I don't want to claim that the two factors that I have discussed—the way in which metaphysical realism has gotten itself into trouble in the twentieth century, and the way in which the doctrine of incommensurability of different languages and even different texts has come to seem coercive to Derrida—are the sole reasons which shape Derrida's eventual deconstructionist position. Certainly there are many other influences, including Heidegger, Marx, Freud, and Nietzsche. But when one looks for *arguments* in and around Derrida's writings to support the radical claims that he repeats over and over, I think one finds that they are related to, on the one hand, Goodman's irrealism[29] and, on the other hand, Saussure's form of the doctrine of incommensurability. While those doctrines are well worth re-flecting on—they do show much that is of interest—they do not justify the extreme philosophical radicalisms of either Good-man or Derrida.

Differences between Goodman and Derrida

Although Goodman and Derrida might both be described as "irrealists", the philosophical morals that they draw from their respective irrealisms are quite different. Although Goodman sees difficulties with the notion of truth, he never proposes that we should give it up. Instead, he proposes that we should widen the range of philosophical discussion. Instead of talking exclu-sively or primarily about language, about versions that consist of statements, we should also consider other "versions" of the world, such as paintings, musical compositions, and so on. (According to Goodman, all works of art function semantically and constitute versions/worlds.) Truth is a predicate which we apply only to statements, and statements occur only in verbal versions of the world, but non-verbal versions can also contribute to understanding and can be right or wrong. Goodman is fully aware that there are no necessary and sufficient conditions that we are at present able to state for either rightness or truth— there is certainly no "algorithm" for either rightness or truth. Moreover, he is aware that any even partial and vague standards that a philosopher might propose will always be controversial. But neither the lack of an algorithm nor the controversial character of such general statements as we are able to make should occasion dismay. Even if we do not have a general characterization of rightness, we have partial characterizations of certain kinds of rightness, as Goodman points out. For deductive validity, we have long had such a partial characterization. (That it is only partial is shown by the Gödel incompleteness theorem.) For inductive validity, Goodman has himself proposed the beginnings of an account, although he is well aware that that account does not constitute a formal inductive logic, in the sense of Rudolf Carnap. Generally Goodman's attitude towards the lack of "standards" for rightness or truth is that it is the job of the philosopher to try to devise standards, if not for truth *simpliciter* or for rightness *simpliciter*, then for rightness and truth in various areas. If those standards are not an algorithm, they can at least be the beginnings of an account. If we don't yet have even the beginnings of an account in many areas, then that shows that there is a great deal of work for philosophers to do. Goodman describes himself as a "constructionalist"; he constantly stresses the idea that the lack of pre-existing standards is a challenge to philosophers, rather than a reason for dismay.

How should philosophers go about constructing standards for different kinds of rightness? They should look at what we already believe about various cases, and try to formulate standards that agree with those beliefs. But they should not be the slaves of their beliefs. As we try to develop standards, we often find that the very activity of trying to formulate principles leads us to change our view about particular cases. We have thus to aim at "delicate mutual adjustment" of standards and individual cases to one another, hoping for something like a Rawlsian "reflective equilibrium" at the end. But what if our own reflective equilibrium is not regarded as a reflective equilibrium by others? Then, Goodman says, we must simply try to "sell" what seems right to us. The criterion of rightness (in philosophy or anywhere else) cannot be universal consent.[30] Goodman is not afraid of incompleteness, and he is not afraid of making normative judgments.

Derrida's attitudes are much harder to make out. Although this is certainly a misinterpretation,[31] his attacks on the "logocentricism" of Western culture have been interpreted by some of his more left-wing followers as licensing an all-out rejection of the very idea of rational justification. These followers interpret Derrida as teaching that logic and standards of rightness are themselves repressive. Freeing ourselves from capitalism is seen as requiring that we free ourselves from notions like rightness and truth. Goodman would be seen as a hopeless reactionary by these people.

In certain ways, one can understand the reasons for this interpretation. Traditional beliefs include much that is repressive (think of traditional beliefs about various races, about women, about workers, about gays). Our "standards" require not only rational reconstruction but criticism. But criticism requires argument, not the abandonment of argument. The view that all the left has to do is tear down what is, and not discuss what might replace it, is the most dangerous politics of all, and one that could easily be borrowed by the extreme right.

Derrida himself is not guilty of this kind of thinking. He has movingly replied to the charge of nihilism: "We can easily see on which side obscurantism and nihilism are lurking when on occasion great professors or representatives of prestigious institutions lose all sense of proportion and control; on such occasions they forget the principles that they claim to defend in their work and suddenly begin to heap insults, to say whatever comes into their heads on the subject of texts that they obviously have never opened, or that they have encountered through mediocre journalism that in other circumstances they would pretend to scorn".[32]

Yet the fact remains that the thrust of Derrida's work is so negative, so lacking in any sense of what and how we should construct, politically or otherwise, that it is difficult to exonerate him complete from responsibility for the effect of his teaching. He himself does not exonerate Nietzsche completely:

> I do not wish to "clear" its author and neutralize or defuse either what might be troublesome in it for democratic pedagogy or "leftist" politics, or what served as "language" for the most sinister rallying cries of National Socialism. On the contrary, the greatest indecency is *de rigueur* in this place. One may even wonder why it is not enough to say: "Nietzsche did not think that," "he did not want that," or "he would have vomited this," that there is falsification of the legacy and interpretative mystification going on here. One may wonder how and why what is so naively called a falsification was possible (one can't falsify just anything), how and why the "same" words and the "same" statements—if they are indeed the same—might several times be made to serve certain meanings and certain contexts that are said to be different, even incompatible.[33]

Commenting on this passage, Richard Bernstein has written:

> I am not suggesting that Derrida's texts are the occasion for "the most sinister rallying cries". It is difficult to imagine any

texts which are more anti-authoritarian and subversive for any (and all) "true believers". But I am asking whether the signatory of these texts bears some responsibility for their reception. If the desire to write "is the desire to perfect a program or a matrix having the greatest potential variability, undecidability, plurivocality, et cetera, so that each time something returns it will be as different as possible", then doesn't the signatory bear some "responsibility" for the divergent and incompatible ways in which the texts are read and heard. One may wonder "how and why" the texts signed by J.D. can be read (or heard) as being nihilistic, obscurantist, self-indulgent logorrhea and (and I have argued) passionate, political, subversive, committed to opening the spaces of differ-ánce and respecting what is irreducibly other. What is it about the texts of Derrida that allows for, indeed invites, this double reading? After all, "one can't falsify just anything".[34]

I would suggest that the bind Derrida is in is the bind those will find themselves in who do not want to be "irresponsible", but who "problematize" the notions of reason and truth themselves, by teaching that, even if they are indispensable, nevertheless they "retain us in the logocentric circle", they have "collapsed", and so forth.

The problem is that notwithstanding certain moments of argument, the thrust of Derrida's writing is that the notions of "justification", "good reason", "warrant", and the like are primarily repressive gestures. And *that* view is dangerous because it provides aid and comfort for extremists (especially extremists of a romantic bent) of all kinds, both left and right. The twentieth century has witnessed horrible events, and the extreme left and the extreme right are both responsible for its horrors. Today, as we face the twenty-first century, our task is not to repeat the mistakes of the twentieth century. Thinking of reason as just a repressive notion is certainly not going to help us to do that.

Derrida, I repeat, is not an extremist. His own political pronouncements are, in my view, generally admirable. But the philosophical irresponsibility of one decade can become the real-world political tragedy of a few decades later. And deconstruction without reconstruction is irresponsibility.

7

Wittgenstein on Religious Belief

Up to this point I have been surveying, and I must admit participating in, the contemporary philosophical wars. But it is time to draw some lessons from this survey. The first one is relatively superficial. It has, indeed, been drawn time and time again from the philosophical wars of different centuries and different generations: that is, the standard methods of the philosopher—careful argument and drawing distinctions—are more successful in showing that a philosophical position is wrong than they are in establishing that any particular philosophical position is right. We have seen, for example, that contemporary theories of reference are unsuccessful, but this much is widely conceded by philosophers who have very different ideas about where to go from here; similarly, we have seen that standard versions of relativism are self-defeating, but again this is widely conceded by philosophers who have different ideas about where to go from here. My own view is that we should not let ourselves fall into either scepticism or relativism with respect to our normative judgments; and I have urged that if we do *not* let ourselves fall into scepticism and relativism with respect to normative judgments, then a great many philosophical issues look different, including philosophical issues about reference. Yet when I am asked *why* I oppose scepticism and relativism and various forms of "non-cognitivism" with respect to the normative, my answer is not that I have some grand metaphysical theory of the essential nature of normativity to offer. Far from having such a theory, I have already indicated that the idea of a sharp cut between "facts" and "values" is deeply wrong. But I have to admit that if a philosopher wants to hold a different view, then there are a variety of different views that can be held and a variety of devices that can be used to make those views consistent, even if I do not find the resulting views plausible, or, to be frank, even intelligible. The fundamental reason that I myself stick to the idea that there are right and wrong moral judgments and better and worse moral outlooks, and also right and wrong evaluative judgments and better and worse normative outlooks in areas other than morality, is not a metaphysical one. The reason is simply that that is the way that we—and I include myself in this "we"—talk and think, and also the way that we are going to go on talking and thinking.

Hume confessed that he left his scepticism about the material world behind as soon as he left his study; and I observe that no matter how sceptical or how relativistic philosophers may be in their conversation, they leave their scepticism or their relativism behind the minute they engage in serious discussion about almost any subject other than philosophy. If the project of describing "the absolute conception of the world", the project of describing "the things in themselves", the project of dividing our common world into what is "really there" and what is "only a projection", has collapsed, then that seems to be all the more reason to take our lives and our practice seriously in philosophical discussion.

A quite different standard of philosophical correctness has been proposed by the influential philosopher David Lewis. Lewis believes that what we should do in philosophy is work out the consequences of alternative metaphysical positions with great care, and not only of our own metaphysical positions, but also the consequences of all the alternative metaphysical positions that have been proposed by others or that we can think of ourselves. He believes that when the consequences of the various metaphysical positions are worked out in sufficient detail, then our intuitions will tell us which consequences are the least counterintuitive; and the position that we should accept is the one which is, on balance, most free of strongly counterintuitive consequences.

Lewis himself employs the method I have described with great care and with great brilliance. Yet it is striking that the positions that he himself defends are almost universally rejected by analytic philosophers, and rejected precisely on the ground that they are counterintuitive. For example, Lewis believes in the real existence of all possible worlds, that is, he believes that there is a real world, just as real as our own, in which the American Revolution failed and America is still a British colony; a real world in which Ghengis Khan established a lasting empire; and so on. The method Lewis recommends was the method of philosophers in the Middle Ages, and very few philosophers after the Middle Ages have been satisfied that this is a method by which one can settle any questions whatsoever. Indeed, Peirce regarded this method—the method of What is Agreeable to Reason, as he called it—as precisely the method that had to be overcome for modern scientific thinking to be born.

Lewis, to be sure, describes this method in a way which sounds very anti-foundationalist: "One comes to philosophy already endowed with a stock of existing opinions. It is not the business of philosophy either to undermine or to justify these preexisting opinions, to any great extent, but only to try to discover ways of expanding them into an orderly system. A metaphysician's analysis of mind is an attempt at systematizing our opinions about mind. It succeeds to the extent that (1) it is systematic, and (2) it respects those of our pre-philosophic opinions to which we are firmly attached."[1] This passage, considered out of context, would lead one to expect that Lewis is an ordinary conceptual analyst and not the throwback to the Middle Ages I just accused him of being; but the context in which it occurs is precisely the chapter defending the doctrine of the *real existence of other possible worlds* that I alluded to. Although Lewis does defend this metaphysical idea as though he were simply accounting for our "opinions", it is clear that much more is involved than that.

Lewis begins by pointing out that we do say things like "there are countless other ways that things could have been". Then he asks:

> But what does this mean? Ordinary language permits the paraphrase: there are many ways things could have been besides the way they actually are. On the face of it, this sentence is an existential quantification. It says that there exist many entities of a certain description, to wit "ways the world could have been". I believe that things could have been different in countless ways; I believe permissible paraphrases of what I believe; taking the paraphrase at face value, I therefore believe in the existence of entities that might be called "ways things could have been". I call them "possible worlds".
>
> I do not make it an inviolable principle to take seeming existential quantifications in ordinary language at their face value. But I do recognize a presumption in favor of taking sentences at their face value, unless (1) taking them at face value is known to lead to trouble, and (2) taking them some other way is known not to. In this case neither condition is met. I do not know any successful argument that my realism about possible worlds leads to trouble, unless you beg the question by saying that it already *is* trouble . . . All the alternatives I know, on the other hand, do lead to trouble. (*Counterfactuals*, p. 85)

The trouble with this argument is that even if one is a realist about "ways the world could have been" (whatever being a "realist" means), one doesn't have to think of a "way" the world could have been as *another* world. And that is how Lewis thinks of it: if someone asks him what a possible world is, his reply is "I can only ask him to admit that he knows what sort of thing our actual world is, and then explain that other worlds are more things of *that* sort, differing not in kind but only in what goes on in them. We call it alone actual not because it differs in kind from all the rest but because it is the world we inhabit" (p. 85). I once (trying, clumsily, to play his own game) asked him why one couldn't say that a "way" the world could be is just a *property*, a characteristic, however complicated, that the whole world could have had, rather than another world of the same sort as our own. Lewis's reply wasn't to cite more things that we ordinarily say, and offer paraphrases of them, in the "analytic" style of the paragraph I just quoted. Rather, he argued that if a "way the world could have been" were a property (a "state description" of the entire world), and in a world with one such property (call it P) the Eiffel Tower would have been exactly five hundred feet tall instead of its actual height, then the property "is a world in which the Eiffel tower is five hundred feet tall"—call it Q—must be entailed by the property P. But how can this be? Lewis asked. If properties are *simples*, then to say that one property P entails another property Q is to assert some kind of a *necessary relation between distinct simples*, and Lewis found this "unintelligible". So one would have to think of properties as themselves *complexes*: but Lewis didn't see how properties could be complexes, for what would they be complexes of?

In spite of Peirce's attacks on the method of What is Agreeable to Reason, I might be willing to listen to this sort of argument if I had the slightest idea of what these intuitions of Lewis's are supposed to be, or why we should trust their deliverances (calling them "opinions" is hardly an answer), or what the significance is of the fact that something appears "intuitive" and something else appears "unintelligible". Of course, if our intuitions are ways of thinking that have real weight in our lives, whether that weight be practical or spiritual, then I can see why we should regard them as important. But the intuitions to which David Lewis himself gives weight—for example, the intuition that if properties are simples, then it is unintelligible how one property can "entail" another property—seem to me very far from having either practical or spiritual significance. Indeed, far from sharing these intuitions, I feel that I don't even understand what they mean.

A very different objection to the idea of taking our lives and our practice seriously in philosophical discussion comes from radical and/or deconstructionist philosophers. These philosophers sometimes regard any talk of preserving ways in which we speak and think and are going to go on speaking and thinking as inherently reactionary. Isn't it precisely the ways that we speak and think—and according to bourgeois philosophy are going to go on speaking and thinking—that have to be overthrown? If the point of this objection is that we have to overthrow any and every notion of reasonableness or warrant or truth, then I have already discussed this idea at the end of the previous chapter. Let me assume instead a radical critic whom I can take seriously; one who perceives correctly that there are many things that are cruel and unjust about present ways of thinking and talking, and who fears that the maxim that I suggested—that we should give weight in philosophy to the ways we think and talk and are going to go on thinking and talking—may be inherently conservative. This critic points to the danger that the prediction that we are going to go on thinking and talking in a certain way may become a self-fulfilling prophecy.

My answer is that the danger is real, but that does not mean that we are doomed to choose between conservativism and an impossible disengagement from our own culture. Ways of thinking and talking that have weight in our lives are connected with and help to constitute ways of living, and certainly the function of philosophers is not simply to endorse existing ways of living; but neither is it to play sceptical games. Refusal to acknowledge our common world does not build a better world. Philosophers have often been the ones to propose new ways of thinking and talking and living; one thinks, for example, of the philosophers who taught us to speak of "the rights of man". But talk of "the rights of man" was itself ambiguous. On the one hand, it could be taken, and was taken, as the slogan of a revolutionary and Utopian politics, a politics that has again and again drenched the earth with blood. On the other hand, "the rights of man" could be taken, and have been taken, as what Kant called regulative ideas, ideals to strive for, and, as Isaiah Berlin and John Rawls have reminded us, to strive to reconcile with one another. The recognition that there are some good things that we want to preserve in present institutions is not incompatible with the recognition that there is much that is intolerable. As Rorty himself has reminded us, the better can be but need not become the enemy of the best.

These remarks may seem irrelevant to the sort of thing that analytical philosophers do. After all, one can think and talk the way we ordinarily think and talk and also believe reference is fixed by evolution, or that reference is fixed by "causal attachment to the world", or that it is fixed metaphysically in the way that David Lewis has urged.[2] Some analytic philosophers, to be sure, are guilty of challenging the ways we think and talk without proposing any really workable better ways[3] of thinking and talking; but most analytic philosopher nowadays consider themselves to be providing something like (or at least "continuous with") a scientific explanation of the success of ordinary ways of thinking and talking. It is this analogy—the analogy of the work of philosophers like Jerry Fodor, or the proponents of "evolutionary intentionality", or the metaphysicians of "possible worlds" to the work of the scientist—that I find fundamentally frivolous. I am not going to argue this here, but in the case of Fodor and the proponents of evolutionary intentionality the discussion in the previous chapters should suffice to convince anyone who knows what a scientific theory, like the theory of evolution, has really accomplished that there is no analogy at all between a serious scientific theory and a typical construction in "analytic metaphysics". Most constructions in analytic metaphysics do not extend the range of scientific knowledge, not even speculatively. They merely attempt to rationalize the ways we think and talk in the light of a scientistic ideology.

But I am growing tired of criticizing the errors of contemporary philosophers, analytic and non-analytic alike. In the rest of this book I want to try to sketch a better way in philosophy. I shall not do that by issuing a blueprint for a new philosophy, or even a manifesto. At the best, blueprints and manifestos always involve a good deal of fantasy, and we have seen enough fantasy in recent philosophy—both the fantasy of being scientific and the fantasy of putting an end to the claims of truth and reason. The only way I know of pointing to a better way in philosophy is to engage in a certain kind of reading, a reading of the work of some philosophers who, in spite of their mistakes and their flaws—and what philosopher does not make mistakes and have flaws?—point the way toward and exemplify the possibility of philosophical reflection on our lives and language that is neither frivolously sceptical nor absurdly metaphysical, neither fantastic parascience nor fantastic parapolitics, but serious and fundamentally honest reflection of the most difficult kind.

I shall begin by discussing Wittgenstein's three Lectures on

Religious Belief.[4] We do not have the full text of these lectures; what we have are notes taken by one of the people who was present. But these notes are a valuable source nonetheless. For one thing, in these lectures Wittgenstein's students sometimes make objections or make suggestions as to what Wittgenstein should say; and Wittgenstein's refusal to accept what his students thought he should say tells us a great deal about Wittgenstein's philosophy, and about the ways in which even the best of his students were tempted to misinterpret it.

I was first led to study the published notes on the Lectures on Religious Belief by their subject, of course, but as I studied them and thought about them it came to seem to me more and more that besides the interest they have for anyone who has thought about the subject of religious language and religious belief, they also have great interest for anyone who is interested in understanding the work of the later Wittgenstein. They were given, in fact, in a transitional period, the summer of 1938, when Wittgenstein's later views were in development, and they by no means bear their meaning on their sleeve. Even if we had the full text of what Wittgenstein said in that room in Cambridge in 1938, I suspect we would be deeply puzzled by these lectures; as it is, we have only twenty-one printed pages of notes summarizing three lectures.

The first of the three lectures sets the interpretative problem before us. What Wittgenstein says in this first lecture is very much contrary to received opinion in linguistic philosophy, and there is an obvious problem as to how it is to be understood. In this lecture, Wittgenstein considers a number of religious utterances, not utterances about God, but about the afterlife, or the Last Judgment, such as "an Austrian general said to someone, 'I shall think of you after my death, if that should be possible' ". (Wittgenstein says, "We can imagine one group would find this ludicrous, another who wouldn't.")[5] Again,

Wittgenstein imagines someone asking him if he believes in a Last Judgment, and on the first page of the published notes Wittgenstein says, "Suppose I say that the body will rot, and another says 'No. Particles will rejoin in a thousand years, and there will be a Resurrection of you.'" Wittgenstein's comment is "If some said: 'Wittgenstein, do you believe in this?' I'd say: 'No.' 'Do you contradict the man?' I'd say: 'No' . . . Would you say: 'I believe the opposite,' or 'There is no reason to suppose such a thing'? I'd say neither."[6] In short—and perhaps this is the only thing that is absolutely clear about these lectures—Wittgenstein believes that the religious man and the atheist talk past one another.

I remember that the first time I had lunch with a great student of comparative religion, Wilfrid Cantwell Smith, Smith said to me that when the religious person says "I believe there is a God" and the atheist says "I don't believe there is a God" they do not affirm and deny the same thing. We shall see that Wittgenstein makes the same point later in his lectures. Religious discourse is commonly viewed (by atheists) as pre-scientific or "primitive" discourse which has somehow strangely—due to human folly and superstition—managed to survive into the age of the digital computer and the neutron bomb. Wittgenstein (and Smith) clearly believe no such thing. Wittgenstein's picture is not that the believer makes a claim and the atheist asserts its negation. It is as if religious discourse were somehow incommensurable, to employ a much-abused word. But there are many theories of incommensurability, and the problem is to decide in what way Wittgenstein means to deny the commensurability or homophony of religious and non-religious discourse.

The first lecture provides us with a number of clues. When a question is an ordinary empirical question, the appropriate attitude is often not to say "I believe" or "I don't believe", but to say, "probably not" or "probably yes" or possibly "I'm not sure". Wittgenstein uses the example of someone's saying "There is a German aeroplane overhead". If Wittgenstein were to reply, "Possibly I'm not so sure", one would say that the two speakers were "fairly near". But what if someone says "I believe in a Last Judgement" and Wittgenstein replies "Well, I'm not so sure. Possibly"? Wittgenstein says, "You would say that there is an enormous gulf between us".[7] For a typical non-believer, the Last Judgment isn't even a possibility.

I don't think that Wittgenstein is denying that there is a state of mind in which someone on the verge of a religious conversion might suddenly stop and say, "What if there is a Last Judgment?". But I think that Wittgenstein would deny that this is at all like "Possibly there is a German airplane overhead."

Wittgenstein distinguishes religious beliefs partly by what he calls their unshakeability. Speaking again of the man who believes in a Last Judgment, Wittgenstein says: "But he has what you might call an unshakeable belief. It will show, not by reasoning or by appeal to ordinary grounds for belief, but rather by regulating for in [sic] all his life. This is a very much stronger fact—foregoing pleasures, always appealing to this picture. This in one sense must be called the firmest of all beliefs, because the man risks things on account of it which he would not do on things which are by far better established for him. Although he distinguishes between things well-established and not well-established".[8]

In understanding these remarks I think it is important to know that although Wittgenstein presents himself in these lectures as a non-believer, we know from the other posthumous writings published as *Culture and Value* that Wittgenstein had a deep respect for religious belief, that he thought a great deal about religious belief, especially about Christianity, and that in particular he paid a great deal of attention to the writings of Kierkegaard, and especially to the *Concluding Unscientific Postscript*. The man who has an unshakeable belief in the Last Judgment and lets it regulate for all his life, although he is very willing to admit that the Last Judgment is not an established fact, sounds like a Christian after Kierkegaard's own heart.[9] Yet Kierkegaard himself wrote that faith "has in every moment the infinite dialectic of uncertainty present with it".[10] It would be ludicrous to suppose that inner struggles with the issue of religious belief are something that Wittgenstein did not know. When he takes the unshakeableness of a religious belief as one of its characteristics, he does not mean that a genuine religious belief is always and at every moment free from doubt. Kierkegaard spoke of faith as a state to be repeatedly reentered, and not as a state in which one can permanently stay. But I think that Kierkegaard would agree with Wittgenstein—and that Wittgenstein is here agreeing with Kierkegaard—that religious belief "regulates for all" in the believer's life, even though his religious belief may alternate with doubt. In this respect it is different from an empirical belief. If I confidently believe that a certain way is the right way to build a bridge, then I will set out building the bridge that way. If I come to have doubts, I will not go on building the bridge in that way (unless I am a crooked contractor); I will halt the construction and run further tests and make calculations.

Wittgenstein uses the following example:

> Suppose you had two people, and one of them, when he had to decide which course to take, thought of retribution and the other did not. One person might, for instance, be inclined to take everything that happened to him as a reward or punishment, and another person doesn't think of this at all.
>
> If he is ill, he may think: "What have I done to deserve

this?" This is one way of thinking of retribution. Another way is, he thinks in a general way whenever he is ashamed of himself: "This will be punished."

Take two people, one of whom talks of his behaviour and of what happens to him in terms of retribution, the other one does not. These people think entirely differently. Yet, so far, you can't say they believe different things.

[Wittgenstein adds] It is this way: if someone said: "Wittgenstein, you don't take illness as a punishment, so what do you believe?"—I'd say: I don't have any thoughts of punishment.

There are, for instance, these entirely different ways of thinking first of all—which needn't be expressed by one person saying one thing, another person another thing.[11]

I think we take this example in the wrong way if we suppose that the person who thinks of his life in terms of retribution is supposed to be what we ordinarily call a religious believer. The example doesn't depend on whether he is or isn't. What Wittgenstein means to bring out by the example is that one's life may be organized by very different pictures. And he means to suggest that religion has more to do with the kind of picture that one allows to organize one's life than it does with expressions of belief. As Wittgenstein says, summing up this example, "What we call believing in a Judgement Day or not believing in a Judgement Day—The expression of belief may play an absolutely minor role".[12]

Wittgenstein also contrasts the basis upon which one forms empirical beliefs and the basis upon which one forms religious beliefs. "Reasons look entirely different from normal reasons" in the religious case. "They are, in a way, quite inconclusive". He contrasts two cases: a person who believes that something that fits the description of the Last Judgment will in fact happen, years and years in the future, and who believes this on the basis of what we would call scientific evidence, and a person who has a religious belief which "might in fact fly in the face of such a forecast and say 'No. There it will break down.'" Wittgenstein says that if a scientist told him that there would be a Last Judgment in a thousand years, and that he had to forgo all pleasures because of such a forecast, that he, Wittgenstein, "wouldn't budge". But the person whose belief in a such a forecast was religious and not scientific "would fight for his life not to be dragged into the fire. No induction. Terror. That is, as it were, part of the substance of the belief."[13]

The quoted passages give some sense of the texture of these notes. What seems most important in this first lecture is the repeated claim that the relation between Wittgenstein (who thoroughly conceals his own struggle with or against religious belief in these lectures) and the believer is not one of contradiction:

> If you ask me whether or not I believe in a Judgement Day, in the sense in which religious people have belief in it, I wouldn't say: "No. I don't believe there will be such a thing." It would seem to me utterly crazy to say this.
> And then I give an explanation: "I don't believe in . . .", but then the religious person never believes what I describe.
> I can't say. I can't contradict that person.
> In one sense, I understand all he says—the English words "God", "separate", etc. I understand. I could say: "I don't believe in this," and this would be true, meaning I haven't got these thoughts or anything that hangs together with them. But not that I could contradict the thing.[14]

At this point, a number of possible interpretations of what Wittgenstein is saying might occur to one. (1) I already mentioned the Kuhnian idea of incommensurability. Perhaps Wittgenstein thinks that religious language and ordinary empirical language are incommensurable forms of discourse. The non-religious person simply can't understand the religious person. (2) The religious person and the non-religious person can understand one another, but the non-religious person is using language literally and the religious person is using it in some non-literal way, perhaps emotively, or to "express an attitude". (3) Ordinary discourse is "cognitive" and the religious person is making some kind of "non-cognitive" use of language. What I shall try to show in the light of these lectures, and especially the third and concluding lecture, is that Wittgenstein regards the first as a useless thing to say, and the second and third as simply wrong.

This will, of course, not solve the interpretative problem, but it will in a sense sharpen it, and make it interesting. If Wittgenstein is not saying one of the standard things about religious language—for example, that it expresses false pre-scientific theories, or that it is non-cognitive, or that it is emotive, or that it is incommensurable—then what is he saying and how is it possible for him to avoid all of these standard alternatives? Still more important, how does he think we, including those of us who are not religious (and I don't think Wittgenstein himself ever succeeded in recovering the Christian faith in which he was raised, although it was always a possibility for him that he might), are to think about religious language? What sort of a model is Wittgenstein offering us for reflection on what is always a very important, very difficult, and sometimes very divisive part of human life?

Superstition, Religious Belief, Incommensurability

In the second lecture Wittgenstein discusses the difference between the use of pictures to represent people, including biblical subjects, such as Noah and the ark, and the use of pictures to represent God. "You might ask this question: 'Did Michelangelo think that Noah in the ark looked like this, and that God creating Adam looked like this?' He wouldn't have said that God or Adam looked as they look in this picture."[15] Interestingly, Wittgenstein says: "In general, there is nothing which explains the meanings of words as well as a picture, and I take it that Michelangelo was as good as anyone can be and did his best, and here is the picture of the Deity creating Adam. If we ever saw this, we certainly wouldn't think this the Deity. The picture has to be used in an entirely different way if we are to call the man in that queer blanket 'God', and so on."[16]

One concern of Wittgenstein's in the first two lectures is to contrast superstition and credulity—which often coexist with religion, to be sure—with religious belief in his sense. (Again, the parallelism with Kierkegaard is striking.) In the first lecture, the example of superstition is a Catholic priest who tries to offer scientific arguments for the truths of religion. Wittgenstein's comment is:

> I would definitely call O'Hara unreasonable. I would say, if this is religious belief, then it's all superstition.
>
> But I would ridicule it, not by saying it is based on insufficient evidence. I would say: here is a man who is cheating himself. You can say: this man is ridiculous because he believes, and bases it on weak reasons.[17]

In the second lecture, Wittgenstein says:

> Suppose I went to somewhere like Lourdes in France. Suppose I went with a very credulous person. There we see blood coming out of something. He says: "There you are, Wittgenstein, how can you doubt?" I'd say: "Can it only be explained one way? Can't it be this or that?" I'd try to convince him that he'd seen nothing of any consequence. I wonder whether I would do that under all circumstances. I certainly know that I would under normal circumstances.

"Oughtn't one after all to consider this?" I'd say: "Come on. Come on." I would treat the phenomenon in this case just as I would treat an experiment in a laboratory which I thought badly executed.[18]

Wittgenstein is concerned to deny any continuity at all between what he considers religious belief and scientific belief. When there is a continuity, and only when there is a continuity, Wittgenstein is willing to use words like "ridiculous", "absurd", "credulous", "superstition".

To come back now to the question of incommensurability. An example might seem to be afforded by Wittgenstein's own thought experiment at the beginning of the first lecture, of imagining two people of whom the first one says "I believe in a Last Judgement" and the second (whom Wittgenstein imagines to be himself) says "Well, I'm not so sure. Possibly." Here Wittgenstein does say "It isn't a question of my being anywhere near him, but on an entirely different plane, which you could express by saying: 'You mean something altogether different, Wittgenstein.' "[19] Now, at the beginning of the *Philosophical Investigation* (§43), Wittgenstein famously (or notoriously) wrote, "For a *large* class of cases—though not for all—in which we employ the word 'meaning' it can be defined thus: the meaning of a word is its use in the language." If, as is too often done, one simply ignores the qualification "though not for all", and ascribes to Wittgenstein the view that meaning can always be defined as use, then it is natural to read this "theory of meaning" back into the statement I just quoted, from the first of the Lectures on Religious Belief, and to take it that when Wittgenstein insists again and again that the religious person and the non-religious person are using words in different ways, then he literally means that the words "I believe in a Last Judgement" have a different meaning for someone who can speak of the Last Judgment as a matter of "probability" and for a religious believer. But Wittgenstein doesn't say this. In the notes we have of the first lecture, it is Wittgenstein's imaginary interlocutor who says "You mean something altogether different, Wittgenstein." Wittgenstein replies to his imaginary interlocutor, "The difference might not show up at all in any explanation of the meaning."[20]

Something lovely happens here. Wittgenstein is often charged with simple-mindedly equating use and meaning. Yet here he imagines an interlocutor who plays the role of the stock "Wittgenstein" and proposes to say that the words "I believe in a Last Judgement" have a different meaning in the two uses (one is, of course, completely imaginary), and the real Wittgenstein reminds the stock "Wittgenstein" that we don't use the word "meaning" that way, that is, that the difference in these two uses is not something that we would ordinarily call a difference in meaning.

Wittgenstein says something more about this toward the end of the same lecture. He points out that as an educated person who has read (and, as we know, has thought deeply about) the religious classics there is a very good sense in which he knows what the religious person means, although there is another sense in which Wittgenstein is inclined to say "I don't know whether I understand him or not": "If Mr. Lewy [Cassimir Lewy, one of the students present at these sessions] is religious and says he believes in a Judgement Day, I won't even know whether to say I understand him or not. I've read the same things as he's read. In a most important sense, I know what he means."[21] Wittgenstein immediately goes on to ask, "If an atheist says: 'There won't be a Judgement Day', and another person says there will, do they mean the same?—Not clear what the criterion of meaning the same is. They might describe the same things. You might say, this already shows that this means the same."[22]

So Wittgenstein is warning us against supposing that talk of "meaning the same" and "not meaning the same" will clarify anything here. In a perfectly ordinary sense of meaning the same, we might say that they do mean the same (although Wittgenstein is still inclined to say "I don't even know whether I should say that I understand him or not"); and to dismiss the question whether the words mean the same, that is, whether the sentence means the same, as of no help here, is precisely to dismiss "incommensurability" talk. That the two speakers aren't able to communicate *because* their words have different "meanings" is precisely the doctrine of incommensurability.

Another familiar move is to say that religious language is "emotive", that is, that it is used to "express attitudes". It might seem possible (at least to some) to read these lectures as holding some version of this doctrine, if it were not for the very end of the third lecture. At that point Wittgenstein returns again to the question of whether he (as a non-believer) should say that he understands the the sentences of the religious person or not:

> Suppose someone, before going to China, when he might never see me again, said to me: "We might see one another after death"—would I necessarily say that I don't understand him? I might say [want to say] simply, "Yes. I *understand* him entirely."
>
> *Lewy:* "In this case, you might only mean that he expressed a certain attitude."
>
> I would say "No, it isn't the same as saying 'I'm very fond of you' "—and it may not be the same as saying anything else. It says what it says. Why should you be able to substitute anything else?
>
> Suppose I say: "The man used a picture."[23]

I want to postpone discussion of the last suggestion for a few moments. The reply to Lewy is extremely interesting. What I take Wittgenstein to be pointing out is that there is a perfectly ordinary notion of expressing an attitude, and what he is doing is contrasting the kind of metaphysical emphasis that non-cognitivists (either about religious language or about ethical language) want to put on the notion of expressing an attitude with the ordinary unemphasized use of that notion. If I am fond of someone, I may express my fondness in a variety of ways, for example, by saying "there's no one like you". In such a case, we might say that I was expressing an attitude, and we can say what the attitude was, namely, I was expressing my fondness for the person. That attitude can be expressed explicitly, by saying "I am very fond of So-and-so". However, Wittgenstein is refusing to say that language is "used to express an attitude" when there is no possibility of replacing the language in question by an explicit expression of the so-called attitude. The reason is not hard to guess. Wittgenstein refuses to turn the distinction between saying something because that is, quite literally, what one means to say, and saying something to express an attitude, into a *metaphysical* distinction. As a metaphysical distinction it makes no sense at all without an appropriate metaphysical notion of a "real fact" (the sort of fact that David Lewis can "take at face value"); and that, evidently, is what Wittgenstein thinks we haven't got. (Compare this with the attempt, discussed in the previous chapter, to draw a distinction between an absolute conception of the world and a fact which is only a fact in "some social world or other", in the case of ethics.) In *The Claim of Reason*, Stanley Cavell suggested that Charles Stevenson, the father of emotivism, wrote as if he had forgotten what ethical arguments sound like.[24] Wittgenstein is saying that Lewy is talking as if he had forgotten what religious language sounds like. The philosophical doctrine of non-cognitivism does not help us to understand what religious discourse is really like any more than the philosophical doctrine of incommensurability does.

What then is Wittgenstein saying? I believe that what Witt-genstein (in company with Kierkegaard) is saying is this: that religious discourse can be understood in any depth only by understanding the form of life to which it belongs.[25] What characterizes that form of life is not the expressions of belief that accompany it, but a way—a way that includes words and pictures, but is far from consisting in just words and pictures—of living one's life, of regulating all of one's decisions. Here the believer, Kierkegaard, would add something that Wittgenstein does not say, but that I think he would agree with: namely, that a person may think and say all the right words and be living a thoroughly non-religious life. Indeed, Kierkegaard insists that a person may think he or she is worshipping God and really be worshipping an idol. (I suspect that this is one of the reasons that Kierkegaard is so much hated by fundamentalists. For Kierkegaard an authentically religious form of life is character-ized by a constant concern that one not replace the idea of God with a narcissistic creation of one's own; and this concern expresses itself in uncertainty as much as in certainty. For Kierkegaard, to be absolutely sure you are "born again" is a sign that you are lost.) What Kierkegaard and Wittgenstein have in common is the idea that understanding the words of a religious person properly—whether you want to speak of un-derstanding their "meaning" or not—is inseparable from un-derstanding a religious form of life, and this is not a matter of "semantic theory", but a matter of understanding a human being.[26]

The Religious Person "Uses a Picture"

Still, Wittgenstein himself does say that the religious person "uses a picture". Is this not a way of saying that religious language is non-cognitive? Indeed, Yvor Smythies seems to share this worry, since he objects toward the very end of the third lecture, "This isn't all he does—associate a use with a picture." Wittgenstein's initial reply is, "Rubbish"—hardly an encouraging response. Wittgenstein goes on to explain that when he says the religious man is using a picture, he does not mean by that anything that the religious person himself would not say:

> *Smythies:* "This isn't all he does—associate a use with a picture."
>
> *Wittgenstein:* Rubbish. I meant: what conclusions are you going to draw? etc. Are eyebrows going to be talked of, in connection with the Eye of God?
>
> "He could just as well have said so and so"—this [remark] is foreshadowed by the word "attitude". He couldn't just as well have said something else.
>
> If I say he used a picture, I don't want to say anything he himself wouldn't say. I want to say that he draws these conclusions.
>
> Isn't it as important as anything else, what picture he does use?
>
> Of certain pictures we say that they might just as well be replaced by another—e.g. we could, under certain circumstances, have one projection of an ellipse drawn instead of another.
>
> [He *may* say]: "I would have been prepared to use another picture, it would have had the same effect. . . ."
>
> The whole *weight* may be in the picture . . .
>
> When I say he's using a picture, I'm merely making a *grammatical* remark: [What I say] can only be verified by the consequences he does or does not draw.
>
> If Smythies disagrees, I don't take notice of this disagreement.
>
> All I wished to characterize was the conventions [*sic*] he wished to draw. If I wished to say anything more I was merely being philosophically arrogant. [27]

"All I wished to characterize was the conventions [consequences] he wished to draw. If I wished to say anything more I was merely being philosophically arrogant." One of the most impressive remarks a great philosopher has ever made in a discussion! Wittgenstein is saying here that to say the religious person is using a picture is simply to describe what we can in fact observe: that religious people do employ pictures, and that they draw certain consequences from them, but not the same consequences that we draw when we use similar pictures in other contexts. If I speak of my friend as having an eye, then normally I am prepared to say that he has an eyebrow, but when I speak of the Eye of God being upon me, I am not prepared to speak of the eyebrow of God. But the impressive thing here is not what Wittgenstein says, but the limit he places on his own observation. Pictures are important in life. The whole weight of a form of life may lie in the pictures that that form of life uses. In his own notes, some of which are republished in the collection *Culture and Value*, Wittgenstein says "It is true that we can compare a picture that is firmly rooted in us to a superstition, but it is equally true that we *always* eventually have to reach some firm ground, either a picture or something else, so that a picture which is at the root of all our thinking is to be respected and not treated as a superstition".[28]

In passing, I should like to say that these remarks seem to go totally against the idea that Wittgenstein was against pictures as such. When Wittgenstein attacks philosophers for being in the grip of a picture, the usual reading of this is that Wittgenstein opposes pictures—that pictures are bad. But Wittgenstein in his lectures[29] during the 1930s repeatedly praises pictures in two ways: he praises them as good ways of explaining the meaning of words (we had an example of this in the first lecture) and, moreover, he speaks of pictures as having "weight", or of pictures' being "at the root of all one's thinking". Evidently, then, if certain philosophers are attacked by Wittgenstein for being in the grip of a picture, we may conclude that what is wrong is not that pictures are bad, but that certain pictures are bad—that there are pictures that should not "grip" one, presumably because they lack any significant "weight", because they are not the sort of pictures which could be at the *root* of all one's thinking.[30]

To return to the subject of religious language, one might still suggest, even though Wittgenstein here does not say that religious language is non-cognitive, because he doesn't "want to say anything that [the religious person] wouldn't say", that he has by implication, at least, said that it is non-cognitive, and one might suggest that this is what Smythies was sensitive to, and what Wittgenstein refused to "take notice of". This suggestion raises issues that I will address in the next chapter.

8

Wittgenstein on Reference
and Relativism

I have been discussing the suggestion that Wittgenstein thought that religious language is non-cognitive (even if he doesn't explicitly say so). But what can "non-cognitive" come to when one suggests that "religious language is non-cognitive"? The traditional realist way to spell out the suggestion that religious language is non-cognitive would be to say that ordinary descriptive terms like "my brother" and "America" and "the Arc de Triomphe" all refer to something, but words used in the religious contexts Wittgenstein discusses do not. Isn't Wittgenstein hinting that when one speaks of the Eye of God or the Last Judgment one is *merely* using a picture, that is to say, one isn't referring to anything?

Well, strangely enough, Wittgenstein interrupts his third lecture to talk about the phenomenon of a thought's being about "my brother in America" (Wittgenstein also speaks of "referring"; that is, he speaks both of the thought as being "about" his brother in America and of words as "referring" or "designating"). Now, there is no indication in these notes as to why Wittgenstein interrupted a lecture on religious belief to discuss this subject. The notes for this lecture fill eight pages of the volume edited by Cyril Barrett, and almost three of these pages are occupied by this discussion of reference. The discussion is set off by extra space before and after, so the editors themselves evidently recognized it as some kind of digression.

Moreover, the textual evidence suggests a digression. What precedes the digression is a question about two phrases, "ceasing to exist" and "being a disembodied spirit". Wittgenstein says, "'When I say this, I think of myself having a certain set of experiences.' What is it like to think of this?" He comes back to this question after what I am calling the digression on reference. But no examples from either religious language or from spiritualism (which Wittgenstein contrasts with religion) occur in this digression. The only example used is thinking of Wittgenstein's "brother in America". Yet I don't think this digression can possibly be an accident. It speaks to just the fear that I suggested may lie behind Smythies' remark, the fear that Wittgenstein is at least hinting at a fundamental difference between religious language and non-religious language, namely that religious language does not refer to (or is not "about") anything. The worry is that in ordinary language we have pictures (and, of course, words) and uses of pictures and words, *and* something beyond the words and pictures, while in religious language we have only pictures and words and uses of pictures and words.

I want to suggest that when Wittgenstein said "Rubbish" in response to Smythies' comment, and then hastily added that all he meant to make was a "grammatical" remark, Wittgenstein's initial impatience is accounted for by the fact that Wittgenstein felt that he had already dealt with the issue Smythies was raising (not on that occasion, but in much of his lecturing and philosophical conversation during the thirties), at least implicitly.

The first point that Wittgenstein makes is one that sounds odd today when there are so many discussions of "causal theories of reference". Wittgenstein is struck by the fact that he can think of his brother in America even though there is no causal interaction between him and his brother taking place now. Indeed, Wittgenstein assumes that we don't even think of reference as a causal relation. Our natural temptation is to think that the intentionality of our words is something given in the experience of thought itself. "If you're asked: 'How do you know that it is a thought of such and such?' the thought that immediately comes to your mind is that of a shadow, a picture. You don't think of a causal relation. The kind of relation you think of is best expressed by 'picture', 'shadow', etc."[1] And Wittgenstein goes on to talk in a way familiar to readers of the *Investigations* about how we simultaneously tend to think of thoughts as mental pictures and to ascribe to them powers that no actual picture could possibly have.

> The word "picture" is even quite all right—in many cases, it is even in the most ordinary sense, a picture. You might translate my very words into a picture.[2]
> But the point is this, suppose you drew this, how do I know it is my brother in America? Who says it is him—unless it is here ordinary similarity?
> What is the connection between these words, or anything substitutable for them, with my brother in America?
> The first idea [you have] is that you are looking at your own thought, and are absolutely sure that it is a thought that so and so. You are looking at some mental phenomenon, and you say to yourself "obviously this is a thought of my brother being in America." It seems to be a super-picture. It seems, with thought, that there is no doubt whatever. With a picture, it still depends on the method of projection, whereas here it seems that you get rid of the projecting relation, and are absolutely certain that this is thought of that.[3]

Wittgenstein is, of course, not thinking of causal theories of the kind put forward by Fodor, or causal theories of the kind sometimes (incorrectly) ascribed to me and to Saul Kripke.[4]

The point he is making is, I think, a phenomenological one: if I am a person in England thinking of my brother in America, then I don't conceive of myself as having some occult kind of causal interaction with my brother in America. That reference is not an ongoing causal interaction is, of course, true on any theory of reference. On the other hand, although Wittgenstein is not thinking about this, he is causally connected to his brother in the sense that he has causally interacted with him in the past, the causal interaction has produced brain traces which have remained in his brain to that day, and so on. And he is "causally connected" to America (even if he had never been in America), in the sense of having acquired the word "America" from people who acquired it from people who acquired it from people . . . who were in America. This story is, of course, very familiar nowadays.

I want to speculate a little about what Wittgenstein might have said about this, because I think it will help us to understand the points he is making both in the brief remarks on reference transcribed in these notes, and at length in *Philosophical Investigations*. But first I will review some points about reference which were familiar to Frege, and in fact familiar to Kant, but which have been neglected, if not completely forgotten, in current discussions of causal theories of reference.

For this purpose, I want to ignore the fact that Fodor's theory doesn't work. Let us imagine that Fodor's theory did work perfectly—that his counterfactuals were all true, and that they provided a necessary and sufficient condition for a word to refer to a kind of thing—or else that somebody else had succeeded in putting forward a definition of reference in terms of "causal attachment". What could possibly remain to say about reference?

Well, the first thing to notice is that—although terms like

"causal theory of reference" may suggest the opposite—nobody actually thinks that *all* cases of referring are cases of causal attachment. It is obvious that we can refer to things that we have not causally interacted with. We can refer to future things, for example, the first baby that will be born after the year 3000. I can refer to things outside my "light cone" altogether,[5] for example, if there are galaxies outside my light cone, I can refer to the nearest such galaxy in a certain direction, and so on. One causal theorist who explicitly takes account of this in various publications is Richard Boyd.[6] Boyd has proposed taking over Russell's distinction between knowledge by acquaintance and knowledge by description, and modifying it in the following way: instead of talking about two kinds of knowledge, we should speak of two kinds of reference, reference by causal connection and reference by description. The idea is that we can refer to things that we are not causally attached to because we can form descriptions of them using terms which do refer via causal attachment.

Another problem—which, as we shall see, is closely related to the problem Boyd addresses—is that the causal connection theory accounts for the reference of individual words but not for the truth of sentences. Even if the word *cat* gets its reference from the fact that cats cause "cat" tokenings, and *mat* gets its reference from the fact that mats cause "mat" tokenings, and "on" gets its reference from the fact that instances of the spatial relation of one thing being on another cause "on" tokenings, how does that account for the fact that the whole sentence "the cat is on the mat" has the truth value it does in various situations?

The relation between these two problems is this: although it is individual words that are causally attached, in the sense of being the termini of the kinds of causal chains that Fodor talks about (of course, other theorists talk about different kinds of causal chains), yet it is somehow groups of words organized by syntactic structures that have truth values. To say that if the parts of a referring expression refer, then obviously the referring expression as a whole will refer, is simply too fast. In one sense, in fact, this is false. If we said that whenever the parts of a referring expression refer *in the sense of being causally attached to a referent*, then the referring expression as a whole will refer *in the very same sense*—that is, in the sense of being causally attached to a referent—then this is false. In the phrase "the first baby born after the year 3000", the word "baby" is causally attached to a kind, that is, the speaker and his language community have had causal interactions with babies in which the "property of being a baby" played a relevant causal role (it hurts me to talk this way, but this is the kind of metaphysical language these people speak!), but the phrase "the first baby born after the year 3000" is not causally attached to its referent in the same way, that is, we have not causally interacted with the first baby born after the year 3000, and the "property of being the first baby born after the year 3000" has not yet had any causal influence on us.

On the other hand, if one says "the word *baby* refers in one way, and that explains why the whole phrase *refers in a different way*", then we need a theory of this different way of referring. Oddly enough, causal theorists don't seem to recognize that any theory is needed here. Hartry Field, for example (who subsequently seems to have moved to an agnostic position with respect to causal theories of reference) suggested in his well-known article on truth many years ago[7] that if we can construct a causal theory of what he called "primitive reference", that is, reference in the case of what would be the primitive terms of English in a suitable formalization of English, then reference in the case of complex expressions can be defined by a Tarski-style recursive definition. Such a definition simply assumes that the result of joining two referring expressions with *and* produces an expression which refers (in a sense which is not explained) to the intersection of the extensions of the two joined referring expressions; that prefixing a negation sign to a referring expression results in a referring expression which refers (in a sense which is not explained) to the complement of the extension of the expression to which the negation sign is prefixed; and so forth. But surely this can't be part of either the meaning or the nature of reference. There is nothing in the nature of reference to make it the case that joining two expressions with *and* results in anything at all. If joining expressions with *and* gives us an intersection of extensions, then this must have something to do with the role of *and* in the language. In short, we need a theory of "reference by description" as much as a theory of primitive reference.

To sum up: if we accept the Boyd-Field distinction between primitive reference and reference by description for the moment, then a theory of primitive reference is not a theory of reference at all. At best it is a definition of a neologism, that is, it is a definition of a concept made up in the hope that it will aid us in giving a theory of reference. Only if we had a definition of primitive reference *and* a theory of reference by description could we possibly be said to have a theory of reference at all, and so far none of the causal theorists has really attempted to give a theory of reference by description.

Here is a way of making the problem clear, a way which, in essence, goes back to Frege and even back to Kant: the sentence "the cat is on the mat" consists of exactly the same words as the mere list, "the", "cat", "is", "on", "the", "mat". Yet the sentence has a truth value, in an appropriate situation, while the list has no truth value. What constitutes the difference between a sentence and a list? The phrase "the first baby born after the year 3000" has a referent, while the list consisting of those words in that order does not refer to anything (unless we say it refers to the words listed). Again, what constitutes the difference? In Kant's terminology, a judgment is not just a series of representations but a "synthesis" of those representations; it was just this problem that led Frege to give priority to sentence meaning over word meaning in his theorizing about language.

The answer to this problem is in one sense quite obvious, or at least it is obvious after Wittgenstein: what makes it the case that a sentence can have a truth value or a complex phrase can have reference, whereas a mere list of words has neither truth value nor reference, is that we *use* sentences and complex phrases in very different ways from the ways in which we use mere lists. This observation totally undercuts the idea of a merely causal theory of reference. Referring, I repeat, is using words in a certain way (or, to anticipate a little bit, in any one of a variety of ways). It may well be that a certain referring use of some words would be impossible if we were not causally connected to the kinds of things referred to; indeed, I believe that this is the case. But that is to say that there are causal constraints on reference, not that the referring *is* the causal connection. No matter how the word *cat* is causally connected to the world, if I say "cat, cat, cat, cat . . ." a hundred times, I am not referring to cats, whereas if I use the word *cat* in certain ways, I am referring to cats.

In his digression on reference, Wittgenstein speaks of what I am calling a referring use of language as a "technique of usage", and he suggests that the illusion of intrinsic intentionality, that is, the illusion that reference is a mysterious something that exists while we think and about which nothing can be said, is due to the fact that we pay attention only to our subjective experience and not to the technique of using the word:

["Is thinking something going on at a particular time, or is it spread over the words?" "It comes in a flash." "Always?—it sometimes does come in a flash, although this may be all sorts of different things.]

If it does refer to a technique, then it can't be enough, in certain cases, to explain what you mean in a few words; because there is something which might be thought to be in conflict with the idea going on from 7 to 7.5, namely the practice of using it [the phrase.]

When we talked of: "So and so is an automaton", the strong hold of that view was [due to the idea] that you could say: "Well, I know what I mean" . . . , as though you were looking at something happening while you said the thing, entirely independent of what came before and after, the application [of the phrase]. It looked as though you could talk of understanding a word, without any reference to the technique of its usage. It looked as though Smythies said he could understand the sentence, and that we then had nothing to say.[8]

At one time, I myself had the hope that what Wittgenstein refers to as the use of words, or in this lecture as the technique of usage, could be completely surveyed and analyzed in a functionalist way; that is, that all the various referring uses of words could be neatly organized and depicted by something like a computer program. In *Representation and Reality*, I explained my reasons for thinking it overwhelmingly likely that this cannot be done. (The difficulties for Artificial Intelligence I described in Chapter 2 are connected with some of those reasons.) But if we cannot survey all the referring uses of words, then there is a sense in which we don't have a *theory* of "the nature of reference" at all (not even if we succeed in showing that our words are causally attached to what they refer to in certain ways). If we cannot give some kind of a scientific theory of the nature of reference, that is, of the referring uses of our words, then how are we to look at reference?

In *Philosophical Investigations* Wittgenstein attacks the idea that one can use a word only if one possesses a necessary and sufficient condition for its application. He uses the word "game" as an example (the example has now become famous), and he says that in the case of that word we don't have a necessary and sufficient condition. We have some paradigms—paradigms of different kinds, in fact—and we extend the word "game" to new cases because they strike us as similar to cases in which we have used it before (he describes this as our "natural reaction"). He speaks of games as forming a family, as having a family resemblance, and he also uses the metaphor of a rope. The rope is made up of fibers, but there is no fiber running the length of the whole rope. There are similarities between one game and another, but there is no one similarity between all games.

While the notion of a family-resemblance word has become commonplace, many people miss Wittgenstein's point: as Rush Rhees emphasized a long time ago,[9] Wittgenstein was not just making a low-level empirical observation to the effect that in addition to words like *scarlet*, which apply to things all of which are similar in a particular respect, there are words like *game* which apply to things which are not all similar in some one respect. Wittgenstein was primarily thinking not of words like *game*, but of words like *language* and *reference*. It is precisely the big philosophical notions to which Wittgenstein wishes to apply the notion of a family resemblance. On Rush Rhees's reading (and I am convinced he is right), what Wittgenstein is telling us is that referring uses don't have an "essence"; there isn't some one thing which can be called referring. There are overlapping similarities between one sort of referring and the next, that is all. This is why, for example, Wittgenstein is not puzzled, as many philosophers are, about how we can "refer" to abstract entities. After all, we are not causally attached to the number three, so how can we refer to it? Indeed, do we know that there is such an object at all? For Wittgenstein the fact is that the use of number words is simply a different use from the use of words like *cow*. Stop calling three an "object" or an "abstract entity" and look at the way number words are used, is his advice.

Now, the relevance of this to a lecture on the philosophy of religion is as follows: just as I have suggested that Wittgenstein would not have regarded talk of incommensurability as helpful, and would not have regarded talk of certain discourses' being "cognitive" and other discourses' being "non-cognitive" as helpful, I suggest that he would not have regarded the question as to whether religious language *refers* as helpful either. (He speaks of a "muddle".) The use of religious language is both like and unlike ordinary cases of reference: but to ask whether it is "really" reference or "not really" reference is to be in a muddle. There is no essence of reference. Religious thinkers will be the first to tell you that when they refer to God, their "referring use" is quite unlike the referring use of "his brother in America". In short, Wittgenstein is telling you what *isn't* the way to understand religious language. The way to understand religious language isn't to try to apply some metaphysical classification of possible forms of discourse.

Wittgensteinian Relativism?

We are by no means at the end of our interpretative quest. Has Wittgenstein simply immunized religious language from all criticism? Has Wittgenstein made it impossible to be an atheist?

Not entirely. First of all, Wittgenstein presents himself as a non-believer in these lectures. As I have pointed out, he had a very respectful attitude toward religious belief; he seems to me, in a way, to have aspired to but not achieved religious belief; he described himself in conversations as having had a "religious temperament". Yet there is little doubt that Wittgenstein was telling us the truth when he said that he himself would never say that he believes that there will be a Last Judgment. Indeed, Wittgenstein says—and the one thing I am convinced of is that he was being quite honest—that he doesn't even know whether to say he *understands* the man who says that he believes there will be a Last Judgment. (And reading more philosophy or more linguistics isn't going to help Wittgenstein decide whether to say he understands or not.)

What is Wittgenstein's attitude toward the other side, that is, toward those who would combat religious belief, fight it fiercely, denounce it? Here we have less to go on. But I will allow myself to speculate. First of all, Wittgenstein does say, in the first lecture, that the line between religious belief and scientific belief is not always sharp, that one cannot think of the two as separated by a chasm. Here Wittgenstein is pretty clearly thinking not of our own society, in which a distinction between science and religion has been institutionalized, but of a so-called primitive society:

> We come to an island and we find beliefs there, and certain beliefs we are inclined to call religious . . . They have sentences, and there are also religious statements.
>
> These statements would not just differ in respect to what they are about. Entirely different connections would make them into religious beliefs, and there can easily be imagined transitions where we wouldn't know for our life whether to call them religious beliefs or scientific beliefs. (p. 58)

I take these remarks of Wittgenstein's as a justification for connecting what Wittgenstein says about religious belief in these three lectures with what he says about the thought of so-called primitive people in his notes on Frazer's *Golden Bough*.[10] In particular, it is clear from those notes that Wittgenstein thinks we tend to approach primitive cultures in a way that is fundamentally supercilious and self-congratulatory; instead of seeing how different the "primitive" language games are from our own, we see them as simply inferior versions of our own. We fail to see the enormous difference between someone who is playing one of our language games and making a blunder, or being stupid, and someone whose form of life is entirely different. In particular, Wittgenstein does not view primitive magic as inferior or failed science. In effect, Wittgenstein accuses us of arrogance, and not just arrogance, but narcissism.

That does not mean that we can never criticize a primitive culture. Here I am going to leave Wittgenstein's Lectures on Religious Belief and turn for the rest of this chapter to his *On Certainty*. Some of his remarks, especially the remarks about the possibility of combating another culture and the difficulty of giving reasons why one combats another culture, have led some people to see Wittgenstein as an out-and-out cultural relativist. I believe that, in fact, Saul Kripke reads these passages in that way, and I think that this may lie behind the reading that Kripke offers us in *Wittgenstein on Rules and Private Language*.

The first thing to notice is that Wittgenstein does occasionally offer criticism of a primitive belief; for example, he describes ordeal by fire as an "absurd" way of reaching a verdict.[11] But what Wittgenstein says in *On Certainty* about combating other forms of life, other language games, could give rise to yet another interpretation of the position taken in the notes on Frazer's *Golden Bough* and in the Lectures on Religious Belief.

Perhaps Wittgenstein just thinks that there are a variety of different possible language games, a variety of possible human forms of life, and there is nothing to be said about the rightness or wrongness of one as opposed to another. Indeed, one might add, Wittgenstein doesn't even think one can choose one as opposed to another, since it is clear that we don't *choose* our form of life in the sense in which Wittgenstein is using "form of life". Strong support for such a reading might seem to come from the following:[12]

§608: Is it wrong for me to be guided in my actions by the propositions of physics? Am I to say that I have no good grounds for doing so? Isn't it precisely this that we call a "good ground"?

§609: Suppose that we met people who did not regard this as a good ground, and who did not regard that as a telling reason. Now how do we imagine this? Instead of the physicist, they consult an oracle. And for that we consider them primitive.

Is it wrong for them to consult an oracle and be guided by it?—If we call this "wrong", aren't we using our language game as a base from which to *combat* theirs?

§610: And are we right or wrong to combat it? Of course there are all sorts of slogans which will be used to support our proceedings.

§611: Where two principles really do meet which cannot be reconciled with one another, then each man declares the other a fool and a heretic.

§612: I said I would "combat" the other man—but wouldn't I give him *reasons?* Certainly, but how far do they go? At the end of reasons comes *persuasion*. (Think what happens when missionaries convert natives.)

This certainly sounds like relativism. (I recall how dismayed I was when I first encountered these paragraphs.) But, on closer reading, the relativist interpretation came to seem less and less supportable. If all we had was §609, then one might say that Wittgenstein was distancing himself from those who say that consulting an oracle is "wrong". It is not clear that the "we" in "if we call this 'wrong', aren't we using our language game as a base from which to *combat* theirs" includes Wittgenstein himself. But this ambiguity is immediately removed in §612, when Wittgenstein says "I said I would 'combat' the other man". So Wittgenstein isn't just an onlooker here. Wittgenstein himself will at least sometimes combat a different language game. Who wouldn't? (What decent person wouldn't combat a language game that involved ordeal by fire, for example?) We cannot suppose that the things that Wittgenstein would say if he were combating another language game (for instance, that it is "absurd" to try to reach a verdict on anything through ordeal by fire) are in some sense not believed by Wittgenstein, or that they are given a special metaphysical reinterpretation by Wittgenstein, for the whole burden of *On Certainty* is that we have no other place to stand but within our own language game. If words like "know", for example, cannot bear a metaphysical emphasis, as Wittgenstein suggests in one place, that is all the more reason for using them where they belong and without that metaphysical emphasis. Wittgenstein simply thinks it absurd to settle questions through ordeal by fire.

Well, what about the rest of §612? I take Wittgenstein here to be simply telling us what is the case: that when we try to argue with, say, the Azande, there are times when we cannot find reasons that are reasons for them; the worldviews are so totally different that we sometimes find that in an argument with an intelligent Azande we cannot resort to ordinary argument based on premises that we share with the Azande but have to resort to persuasion.

But what interests me far more than §612 is the tone of §610 and §611. Wittgenstein has said (§605) that he would combat ordeal by fire, and here makes it clear that he would combat the use of an oracle to make the sorts of predictions that we use physics to make. But the reference to "all sorts of slogans" ["allerlei Schlagworten (Slogans)"] and the statement in §611 that "each man declares the other a fool and a heretic" have, to my ear, a tone of distaste about them. If I am right in reading the Lectures on Religious Belief in juxtaposition with Wittgenstein's notes on Frazer's *Golden Bough*, then Wittgenstein wants us to stop and think about *when* we should combat a religious language game or a primitive language game which is not ours or our culture's. If we view other language games as simply stupid or ignorant forms of our own language games, we will be constantly combating and we will be constantly failing to *see*. If we see more accurately, we may find that there are fewer language games that we want to combat. But even when we do combat, and Wittgenstein does sometimes join us in combating, we don't have to scream "Fool!" and "Heretic!"

Elizabeth Anscombe[13] once asked Ludwig Wittgenstein what he would do if a friend of his believed in faith healing; would he try to talk him out of it? And Wittgenstein replied that he would, but he didn't know why. (In conversation, Saul Kripke once cited this to me as clear evidence that Wittgenstein was a relativist.) I take it that Wittgenstein did not mean, by what he said to Elizabeth Anscombe, that he does not know that sulfa drugs or penicillin are more effective in treating bacterial pneumonia than faith healing is. The point is rather that this is a perfectly useless thing to say to the man who believes in faith healing (it is a premise he doesn't share), and Wittgenstein was, I think, recoiling from using *allerlei Schlagworten*. Slogans may be part of our language game, but they are by no means the best or noblest part.

Still, what are we to say to the reader who takes these passages as showing that Wittgenstein thought that language games are simply irrational, arbitrary facts of nature? Is such a reading not supported by the following?

§559: You must bear in mind that the language game is so to say something unpredictable. I mean it is not based on grounds. It is not reasonable (or unreasonable).
It is there—like our life.

In German, the next-to-last sentence reads "Nicht vernünftig (oder unvernünftig)". I cite the German here, because the German *vernünftig* has a somewhat different flavor from the English "reasonable". "The language game is not reasonable" suggests that it is not based on reasons, and while this is certainly true, I do not think that this is the point, or at least not the only point, that Wittgenstein is making here. In German the word *vernünftig* connects with *Vernunft*, and this particular notion of Reason was given pride of place by Kant, who contrasted Reason in that sense with mere understanding, *Vernunft* with *Verstand*. (In the tradition that comes from Hume, on the other hand, *reason* and *reasonableness* were contrasted; Hume tells us that reason cannot show that the sun will rise tomorrow, but it would be most *unreasonable* not to expect it to.) I am inclined to read Wittgenstein in §559 as saying that the language game is like our life in that neither the language game nor our life is based on *Vernunft*, which is a direct denial of the heart of Kant's philosophy. For Kant human life and human language are distinguished precisely by the unique transcendental capacity that Kant calls *Vernunft*. Wittgenstein does not deny that we understand things and that we reason; indeed, the whole of *On Certainty* is a discussion of when we can and when we can't speak of understanding something, knowing something, showing something, having a reason for something, being certain of something, and so on. But, like John Dewey, whose work I will discuss in the next chapter, Wittgenstein has a naturalistic (but not a reductionist) view of man. We are not mere animals, but our capacities for understanding and for reasoning are capacities which grow out of more primitive capacities which we share with animals (Dewey spoke of "bio-social continuity" in this connection). This naturalistic premise of Wittgenstein's is explicitly stated at §475: "I want to regard man here as an animal. As a primitive being to which one grants instinct but not ratiocination. As a creature in a primitive state. Any logic good enough for a primitive means of communication needs no apology for us. Language did not emerge from some kind of ratiocination."

"I want to regard man here as an animal" refers only to the discussion at that particular point in *On Certainty;* but what follows is a general statement of Wittgenstein's naturalism. Given that naturalism, the claim that the language game is not *vernünftig* or *unvernünftig* seems straightforward. Human life is not the empirical manifestation of the transcendental capacity of reason.

Still, *vernünftig* also has a colloquial use very similar to the colloquial use of the English *reasonable.* (I am not quibbling with the translation here.) Isn't there a sense in which we do think that our language game, or a good deal of it, is "reasonable"? Isn't the language game of physics a very reasonable language game, given its goals? Indeed, isn't even the existence of a language game which enables one to tell someone else that one is hungry and thirsty very reasonable? In a sense, I have already answered this objection; the need to communicate in order to satisfy one's hunger and thirst is just the sort of need that Wittgenstein is thinking of at §475. And the kind of reasoning that we see in physics is a later development, a development within language, not a development which makes language possible.

But let me restate the question. The question, as I wish to put it, is: Can we accept what Wittgenstein tells us in the passages I quoted and not go all the way to relativism? Isn't the conclusion from what has been said that when we "combat" the tribe that uses an oracle to make predictions about matters which physics can deal with, or when we combat the tribe which uses ordeal by fire, the scientific things we say are just "true in our language game" but not "true in their language game" (or "warranted in our language game" but not "warranted in their language game", or "reasonable in our language game" but something else in their language game)? Or better, don't *our* words "true", "warranted", "reasonable" just mean "true in our language game", "warranted in our language game", "true in our language game"?

The reason that this cannot be what Wittgenstein is saying is that to say that it is true in my language game that you are reading this book is not to say that you are reading this book; to say that it's true in my language game that I am eating dinner is not to say that I am eating dinner; and Wittgenstein was obviously aware of this. To say something is true in a language game is to stand outside of that language game and make a comment; that is not what it is to play a language game. Whatever it is that makes us want to replace moves like saying "it's true" or "it's reasonable" or "it's warranted" by "it's true in my language game" or "it's reasonable in my language game" or "it's warranted in my language game" (or makes us want to do this when we see that the language game itself is not grounded on Reason) is something that makes us want to *distance* ourselves from our own language game. It is as if the recognition that our language game does not have a transcendental justification made us want to handle it with kid gloves, or to handle it from a metalanguage. But why is the metalanguage any more secure?

It is important to see that the attraction of relativism doesn't come from its offering us a coherent position from which we can make sense of how we can use language without having a metaphysical foundation; on the contrary, it has often been pointed out[14] that as soon as one tries to state relativism as a *position* it collapses into inconsistency or into solipsism (or perhaps solipsism with a "we" instead of an "I"). The thought that everything we believe is, at best, only "true in our language game" isn't even a coherent thought: is the very existence of our language then only "true in our language game"? So our language game is a fiction?

I think that we get a better understanding of this situation if we see relativism not as a cure or a relief from the malady of "lacking a metaphysical foundation", but rather see relativism *and* the desire for a metaphysical foundation as manifestations of the same disease. The thing to say to the relativist is that some things are true and some things are warranted and some things are reasonable, but of course we can only *say* so if we have an appropriate language. And we do have the language, and we can and do say so, even though that language does not itself rest on any metaphysical guarantee like Reason.

What does it rest on? Wittgenstein gives a shockingly simple answer: trust.

§508: What can I rely on?
§509: I really want to say that a language game is only possible if one trusts something. (I did not say "can trust something").

Our language game rests not on proof or on Reason but *trust*. Something in us finds this thought hard to bear. How hard we find it to bear, and how we wriggle and turn in search of either a transcendental guarantee or a sceptical escape, is something that Stanley Cavell has traced beautifully in a series of books, starting with *The Claim of Reason*. Cavell sees all of Wittgenstein's work as concerned with the problematic of scepticism, but scepticism in a very wide sense. The sceptic in Cavell's enlarged sense may indeed not be a sceptic in the usual sense at all. Rather than professing to doubt everything or to relativize everything, he may claim to have a grand metaphysical solution to all of our problems. But for Cavell the pretense that there is a grand metaphysical solution to all of our problems and sceptical or relativistic or nihilistic escape are symptoms of the same disease. The disease itself is the inability to accept the world and to accept other people, or, as Cavell says, to acknowledge the world and to acknowledge other people, without the guarantees. Something in us both craves more than we can possibly have and flees from even the certainty that we do have.

It is not that relativism and scepticism are unrefutable. Relativism and scepticism are all too easily refutable when they are stated as positions; but they never die, because the attitude of alienation from the world and from the community is not just a theory, and cannot be overcome by purely intellectual argument. Indeed, it is not even quite right to refer to it as a disease; for one of Cavell's points is that to wish to be free of scepticism is also a way of wishing to be free of one's humanity. Being alienated is part of the human condition, and the problem is to learn to live with both alienation and acknowledgment.[15]

I have devoted this much time to the thought of Ludwig Wittgenstein because I think that he gives us an example of how philosophical reflection can be something other than creating new tempests in old teapots, or finding new teapots to create tempests in. At its best, philosophical reflection can give us an unexpectedly honest and clear look at our own situation, not a "view from nowhere" but a view through the eyes of one or another wise, flawed, deeply individual human being. If

Wittgenstein wants to make a bonfire of our philosophical vanities, this is not a matter of sheer intellectual sadism; if I am reading Wittgenstein correctly, those vanities, in his view, are what keep us from trust and, perhaps even more important, keep us from compassion.

9

A Reconsideration of Deweyan Democracy

I know of no better way to close this work than to discuss a philosopher whose work at its best so well illustrates the way in which American pragmatism (at *its* best) avoided both the illusions of metaphysics and the illusions of scepticism: John Dewey. One concern informed all of Dewey's vast output; even what seem to be his purely epistemological writings cannot be understood apart from it. That is Dewey's concern with the meaning and future of democracy. What I want to select for attention from Dewey's thought is a philosophical justification of democracy that I believe one can find in his work. I shall call it the *epistemological justification of democracy* and, although I shall state it in my own words, I shall deliberately select terms from Dewey's own philosophical vocabulary.

The claim, then, is this: Democracy is not just one form of social life among other workable forms of social life; it is the precondition for the full application of intelligence to the solution of social problems.

At the beginning of *Ethics and the Limits of Philosophy*, Bernard Williams draws a very useful distinction between two senses in which one might attempt to justify ethical claims. The more Utopian sense is the following: one might try to find a justification for ethical claims which would actually convince the sceptic or amoralist and persuade him to change his ways.

Williams rightly concludes that this is an unrealistic objective. He then continues: "If, by contrast, the justification is addressed to a community that is already an ethical one, then the politics of ethical discourse, including moral philosophy, are significantly different. The aim is not to control the enemies of the community or its shirkers, but, by giving reason to people already disposed to hear it, to help in creating a community continually held together by that same disposition."[1]

The conception of moral philosophy that Williams suggests here seems to me to have been exactly Dewey's conception. Yet Williams' book ignores not only the historical figure John Dewey, but the very possibility of the justification that Dewey gave. When Williams comes to discuss strategies of justification based on conceptions of human flourishing, "human flourishing" gets taken in an entirely individualistic sense. For example, Williams writes, "On Aristotle's account a virtuous life would indeed conduce to the well-being of the man who has had a bad upbringing, even if he cannot see it. The fact that he is incurable, and cannot properly understand the diagnosis, does not mean that he is not ill" (*Ethics*, p. 40). An objective justification, in the only sense that Williams considers possible, is one that could be given to each human being who is not "ill". In short, the only hope for an objective foundation for ethics[2] that Williams considers is what we might call a "medical" justification—an objective justification for ethics would show that in some non-question-begging sense of "ill", the amoral and/or immoral man is ill. The only place that such a justification could come from, according to Williams, would be "some branch of psychology", and Williams is sceptical about that possibility, although he says that "it would be silly to try to determine *a priori* and in a few pages whether there could be such a theory".[3] The aim mentioned earlier, "not to control the enemies of the community or its shirkers, but, by giving reason to people already disposed to hear it, to help in continually creating a community held together by that same disposition", has been given a radically individualistic interpretation.

However, when Williams explains why it is unlikely that there will ever be a "branch of psychology" which will provide us with objective foundations for ethics, he makes a very interesting remark: "There is . . . the figure, rarer perhaps than Callicles supposed, but real, who is horrible enough and not miserable at all but, by any ethological standard of the bright eye and the gleaming coat, dangerously flourishing. For people who want to ground the ethical life in psychological health it is somewhat of a problem that there can be such people at all."[4] Note the reference to "any ethological standard of the bright eye and the gleaming coat". In Williams' view, an objective standard of human flourishing would regard us as if we were tigers (or perhaps squirrels). Bernard Williams, at least at this moment, is thinking of a standard of human flourishing that ignores everything that Aristotle himself would have regarded as typically human. Dewey, on the other hand, is thinking of us primarily in terms of our capacity intelligently to initiate action, to talk, and to experiment.

Dewey's justification is not only a social justification—that is, one which is addressed to *us* as opposed to being addressed to each "me"—it is also, as I said at the outset, an *epistemological* justification, and this too is a possibility that Williams ignores. The possibility that Williams considers is a "medical" justification; a proof that if you are not moral then you are in some way ill. If we tried to recast Dewey's justification in such terms, then we would have to say the society which is not democratic is in a certain way ill; but the medical metaphor is, I think, best dropped altogether.

The Noble Savage and the Golden Age

Although John Dewey's arguments are largely ignored in contemporary moral and political philosophy, his enterprise—of
justifying democracy—is alive and well. John Rawls's monu-
mental *A Theory of Justice*, for example, attempts to produce
both a rationale for democratic institutions and a standpoint
from which the failures of those institutions can be criticized;
this could also serve as a description of Dewey's project. But
outside of philosophy, and to some extent even inside philosophy, there are those for whom the very enterprise of justifying
democracy is wrong-headed. One sort of objection comes from
anthropologists and other social scientists, although it is by no
means limited to them. A case I have in mind is an essay by
Stephen Marglin and Frédérique Marglin, a radical economist
and a radical anthropologist.[5] These writers reject the idea that
we can criticize traditional societies even for such sexist practices as female circumcision. The Marglins defend their point
of view in part by defending cultural relativism; but besides
their extreme relativism, I think there is something else at
work—something which one finds in the arguments of many
social scientists who are not nearly as sophisticated as the Marglins. Not to be too nice about it, what I think we are seeing
is the revival of the myth of the noble savage. Basically, traditional societies are viewed by these thinkers as so superior to
our own societies that we have no right to disturb them in any
way. To see what is wrong with this view, let us for the moment
focus on the case of sexual inequality in traditional societies.

It is important in discussing this to separate two questions:
the question of paternalistic intervention and the question of
moral judgment, moral argument, and persuasion. It is no part
of Dewey's view, for example, that benevolent despots should
step in wherever there are social ills and correct them:

The conception of community of good may be clarified by reference to attempts of those in fixed positions of superiority to confer good upon others. History shows that there have been benevolent despots who wish to bestow blessings on others. They have not succeeded, except when their actions have taken the indirect form of changing the conditions under which those live who are disadvantageously placed. The same principle holds of reformers and philanthropists when they try to do good to others in ways which leave passive those to be benefited. There is a moral tragedy inherent in efforts to further the common good which prevent the result from being either good or common—not good, because it is at the expense of the active growth of those to be helped, and not common because these have no share in bringing the result about. The social welfare can be advanced only by means which elicit the positive interest and active energy of those to be benefited or "improved". The traditional notion of the great man, of the hero, works harm. It encourages the idea that some "leader" is to show the way; others are to follow in imitation. It takes time to arouse minds from apathy and lethargy, to get them to thinking for themselves, to share in making plans, to take part in their execution. But without active cooperation both in forming aims and in carrying them out there is no possibility of a common good.[6]

Those who object to *informing* the victims of sexual inequality—or of other forms of oppression wherever they are to be found—of the injustice of their situation and the existence of alternatives are the true paternalists. Their conception of the good is basically "satisfaction" in one of the classic Utilitarian senses; in effect they are saying that the women (or whoever the oppressed may be) are satisfied, and that the "agitator" who stirs them up is the one who is guilty of creating dissatisfaction. What the radical social scientists I mentioned are in fact proposing is what Karl Popper has called an "immunizing strategy", a strategy by which the rationales of oppression in other cultures can be protected from criticism. This is based on the idea that the aspirations to equality and dignity are confined to citizens of Western industrial democracies. The events of Tienanmen Square in the spring of 1989 are a more powerful refutation of the view than any words I could write here.

At the other extreme, at least politically, from the "noble savage" argument against attempting to justify democratic institutions is an argument that I seem to detect in the recent writings of Alasdair MacIntyre.[7] In these books, MacIntyre gives a sweeping philosophical résumé of the history of Western thought which does indeed endorse the idea that one system of ethical beliefs can "rationally defeat" another system; which does indeed insist that there can be progress in the development of worldviews; but which is haunted by the suggestion that that progress fundamentally stopped somewhere between the twelfth and fourteenth centuries, and that we have been retrogressing ever since.

If I am disturbed by the suggestion that I describe as haunting MacIntyre's writing, the suggestion that we have been retrogressing ever since the late Middle Ages (a suggestion that has been put forward in a much more blatant way in Allan Bloom's best-seller, *The Closing of the American Mind*), it is because the politics which such views can justify are nothing less than appalling.

What the defenders of the Noble Savage and the defenders of the Golden Age have in common is that their doctrines tend to immunize institutionalized oppression from criticism. The immunizing strategies are different, but they have this in common: they abandon the idea that it would be good for the victims of oppression to know of alternative ways of life, alternative conceptions of their situation, and to be free to try for themselves which conception is better. Both Noble Savagers and Golden Agers block the path of inquiry.

Dewey's Metaphysics (or Lack Thereof)

From what premises does Dewey derive the claim that I imputed to him, that is, the claim that democracy is a precondition for the full application of intelligence to the solution of social problems? As we shall shortly see, the underlying "premises" are some very commonplace assumptions.

Dewey believes (as we all do, when we are not playing the sceptic) that there are better and worse resolutions to human predicaments—to what he calls "problematical situations". That this is so is not something Dewey argues on a priori grounds.[8] But neither are Dewey's premises drawn from some branch of psychology. Here it is instructive to recall Peirce's (as well as Dewey's) arguments for the scientific method itself: in the two famous articles in *Popular Science Monthly* in which Peirce launched the pragmatist movement,[9] he argued that we have learned from experience that the method of authority, the method of tenacity, and the method of What Is Agreeable to Reason don't work. In a similar vein, Dewey's *Logic* conceives of the theory of inquiry as a product of the very sort of inquiry that it describes: *epistemology is hypothesis.*[10] In short, Dewey believes that even if we cannot reduce the scientific method to an algorithm, *we have learned something about how to conduct inquiry in general, and that what applies to intelligently conducted inquiry in general applies to ethical inquiry in particular.*

This would not be the view of the scientistic metaphysicians I have been criticizing. In their view, one cannot suppose that intelligent people are able to tell better resolutions to problematical situations from worse (after experimentation, reflection, and discussion); one first has to show "ontologically" that there is a "fact of the matter" about better and worse resolutions to problematical situations. This is, for example, what bothers Bernard Williams; for Bernard Williams the only way in which there could be facts about what forms of social life are better and worse would be if such facts issued from "some branch of psychology". Lacking such a branch of psychology (and Williams thinks it very unlikely there will ever be one) we have no basis for believing that one form of social life *can be* better than another unless the judgment of better or worse is admitted to express only a "local" truth, a truth in a language game which presupposes the interests and practices of "some social world or other". For Williams the distinction between facts which are "local" in this way and facts which are "absolute" is omnipresent; there can not be "absolute" facts of the kind Dewey thinks intelligent people are able to discover. Dewey, as I read him, would reply that the whole notion of an "absolute" fact is nonsensical.

However, it is a fact about analytic philosophy that, while at one time (during the period of logical positivism) it was an anti-metaphysical movement, it has recently become the most pro-metaphysical movement on the world philosophical scene. From a metaphysical realist point of view, one can never begin with an epistemological premise that *people are able to tell whether A or B;* one must first show that, in "the absolute conception of the world", there are such possible facts as A and B. A metaphysical-reductive account of what good is must precede any discussion of what is better than what. In my view, the great contribution of Dewey was to insist that we neither have nor require a "theory of everything", and to stress that what we need instead is insight into how human beings resolve problematical situations:

[Philosophy's] primary concern is to clarify, liberate, and extend the goods which inhere in the naturally generated functions of experience. It has no call to create a world of "reality" *de novo,* nor to delve into secrets of Being hidden from common sense and science. It has no stock of information or body of knowledge peculiarly its own; if it does not always become ridiculous when it sets up as a rival of science, it is only because a particular philosopher happens to be also, as a human being, a prophetic man of science. Its business is to accept and to utilize for a purpose the best available knowledge of its own time and place. And this purpose is criticism of beliefs, institutions, customs, policies with respect to their bearing upon good. This does not mean their bearing upon *the* good, as something itself formulated and attained within philosophy. For as philosophy has no private store of knowledge or of methods for attaining truth, so it has no private access to good. As it accepts knowledge of facts and principles from those competent in science and inquiry, it accepts the goods that are diffused in human experience. It has no Mosaic or Pauline authority of revelation entrusted to it. But it has the authority of intelligence, of criticism of these common and natural goods.[11]

The need for such fundamental democratic institutions as freedom of thought and speech follows, for Dewey, from requirements of scientific procedure in general: the unimpeded flow of information and the freedom to offer and to criticize hypotheses. Durkheim offered similar arguments up to a point, but came to the conclusion that political opinions should rest on "expert opinion", those without expertise being required to defer to the authority of the experts (and especially to sociologists).[12] While Dewey may not have known of Durkheim's essay, he did consider and reject this view, and he did so for frankly empirical reasons: "A class of experts is inevitably so removed from common interests as to become a class with private interests and private knowledge, which in social matters is not knowledge at all."[13] Here Dewey links up with another of his themes, that privilege inevitably produces cognitive distortion: "All special privilege narrows the outlook of those who possess it, as well as limits the development of those not having it. A very considerable portion of what is regarded as the inherent selfishness of mankind is the product of an inequitable distribution of power—inequitable because it shuts out some from the conditions which direct and evoke their capacities, while it produces a one-sided growth in those who have privilege" (Dewey and Tufts, *Ethics*, pp. 385–386). Thus, if a value as general as the value of democracy is to be rationally defended in the way Dewey advocates, the materials to be used in the defense cannot be circumscribed in advance. There is no one field of experience from which all the considerations relevant to the evaluation of democracy come.

The dilemma facing the classical defenders of democracy arose because all of them presupposed that we already know our nature and our capabilities. In contrast, Dewey's view is that we don't know what our interests and needs are or what we are capable of until we actually engage in politics. A corollary of this view is that there can be no final answer to the question of how we should live, and therefore we should always leave it open to further discussion and experimentation. That is precisely why we need democracy.

At the same time, we do know that certain things stunt our nature and capacities. Dewey was well aware that equality and freedom can conflict, and that there is no easy solution when they do conflict; but he would, I think, feel that this conflict is too much emphasized in present-day political philosophy. In Dewey's view, there is simply no doubt that *inequality*, on the scale that exists today, stunts our nature and capacities, and thus leads to unfreedom on a massive scale. If we are to talk about "conflicts between equality and freedom", we should also talk about the ways in which inequality leads to unfreedom.

Dewey and James

While Dewey's social philosophy is overwhelmingly right, as far as it goes, his moral philosophy is less satisfactory when we try to apply it to individual existential choices. To see why, consider the famous example of an existential choice that Sartre employed in his *Existentialism and Humanism*.[14] It is World War II, and Pierre has to make an agonizing choice between joining the Resistance, which means leaving his aging mother alone on the farm, or staying and taking care of his mother, but not helping to fight the enemy. One of the reasons that Dewey's recommendation to use intelligently guided experimentation in solving ethical problems does not really help in such a case is Dewey's consequentialism. Pierre is not out to "maximize" the good, however conceived, in some global sense; he is out to do what is *right*. Like all consequentialist views, Dewey's has trouble doing justice to considerations of right. I am not saying that Dewey's philosophy never applies to individual existential choices. Some choices are just *dumb*. But Pierre is not dumb. Neither of the alternatives he is considering is in any way stupid. Yet he cannot just flip a coin.

There are, of course, problems of individual choice which can be handled just as one should handle social problems. If, for example, I am uncertain as to which school my child should attend, I may decide to experiment. I may send the child to a school with the idea that if it doesn't work out, I can take her out and put her in a different school. But that is not the sort of problem that Pierre faces.

What some philosophers say about such a situation is that the agent should look for a policy such that if everyone in a similar situation were to act on that policy the consequences would be for the best, and then do that. Sometimes that is reasonable; but in Pierre's situation it isn't. One of the things that is at stake in Pierre's situation is his need to decide who Pierre *is*. Individuality is at stake; and individuality in this sense is not just a "bourgeois value" or an Enlightenment idea. In the Jewish tradition one often quotes the saying of Rabbi Susiah, who said that in the hereafter the Lord would not ask him "Have you been Abraham?" or "Have you been Moses?" or "Have you been Hillel?" but "Have you been Susiah?" Pierre wants to be Pierre; or, as Kierkegaard would say, he wants to "become who he already is". This is not the same thing as wanting to follow the "optimal policy"; or perhaps it is—perhaps the optimal policy in such a case is, in fact, to become who you already are. But doing that is not something that the advice to use the "scientific method" can help you very much with, even if your conception of the scientific method is as generous as Dewey's.

There are various possible future continuations of Pierre's story, no matter what decision he makes. Years afterward, if he survives, Pierre may tell the story of his life (rightly or wrongly) depicting his decision (to join the Resistance or to stay with his mother) as clearly the right decision, with no regrets or doubts about it, whatever the costs may have turned out to be. Or he may tell his story depicting his decision as the wrong decision, or depicting it as a "moral dilemma" to which there was no correct answer.[15] But part of the problem Pierre faces at the time he has to make the decision is that he doesn't even know that what he faces *is* a "moral dilemma" in that sense.

It was precisely this sort of situation that William James was addressing when he wrote the famous essay "The Will to Believe" (which James later said should have been titled "The *Right* to Believe"). Although this essay has received a great deal of hostile criticism, I believe that its logic is, in fact, precise and impeccable; but I will not try to defend that claim here. For James it is crucial for understanding situations like Pierre's that we recognize at least three of their features: that the choice Pierre faces is "forced", that is, these are the only options realistically available to him; that it is "vital"—it matters deeply to him; and that it is not possible for Pierre to decide what to do on intellectual grounds. In such a situation—and *only* in such a situation—James believes that Pierre has the right to believe and to act "in advance of the evidence". The storm of controversy around "The Will to Believe" was largely occasioned by the fact that James took the decision to believe or not to believe in God to be a decision of this kind. Because religious (and, even more, anti-religious) passions are involved, most of the critics do not even notice that the argument of "The Will to Believe" is applied by James and is *meant* to apply to existential decisions of the Pierre type (this is clear not only from the essay itself, but from many other essays in which James offers similar arguments). It is also not noticed that it is meant to apply to the individual's choice of a philosophy, including pragmatism itself.[16]

James believed, as Wittgenstein did, that religious belief is neither rational nor irrational but *arational*. It may, of course, not be a live option for you, because you are either a committed atheist or a committed believer. But if it is a live option for you, then you may be in a situation completely analogous to the one Sartre imagines (or so James believed). The need to believe "in advance of the evidence" is not confined to religious decisions and existential decisions, for James. It plays an essential role in science itself. Although this assertion is hardly controversial nowadays, it was, according to the testimony of someone present,[17] what caused the most controversy when the lecture "The Will to Believe" was repeated for the graduate students at Harvard University. A very nice example of the will to believe in science was related to me recently by Gerald Holton: Max Planck was an early convert to Einstein's theory of (special) relativity, and played an absolutely crucial role in getting that theory the attention of elite physicists. Holton tells me that the physicists in Berlin met with Planck on one occasion and drove him to the wall with their demand that he provide an experimental reason for preferring Einstein's theory over Poincaré's. But Planck could not do this. Instead he said, "Es ist mir eigentlich mehr sympathisch" (It's simply more sympatico to me). Another example is Einstein's own passionate belief in his own general theory of relativity. In a letter to someone, Einstein answered the question of what he would have said if the eclipse experiment had turned out the wrong way by saying, "I would have felt sorry for the Lord God."

James's point was not just a point about the history of science, although he was quite right about that. His claim—which paradoxically the logical positivists helped to make part of conventional philosophy of science with their sharp distinction between context of discovery and context of justification—was that science would not progress if we insisted that scientists never believe or defend theories except on sufficient evidence. When it comes to the institutional decision, the decision by academically organized science, to accept a theory or not, then it is important that we apply the scientific method. In the context of justification (although James did not use that jargon) James was all on the side of scrupulous attention to evidence. But James recognized, before logical positivism appeared, that there is another moment in scientific procedure, the discovery moment, and that in that context the same constraints cannot be applied.

The situation with respect to religion is, of course, quite different. Even though the physicist or the molecular biologist who invents a theory, or other advocates who find the theory *sympathisch*, may believe the theory ahead of the evidence, eventual acceptance by the scientific community depends on public confirmation. In the case of religious belief however— *pace* Alisdair MacIntyre—there is never public confirmation. Perhaps the only one who can "verify" that God exists is God himself.[18] The Pierre case is still a third kind of case. In that case, as I already remarked, Pierre may come to feel afterward that he made the right choice (although he will hardly be able to "verify" that he did), but there is no guarantee that he will. James would say that what these cases have in common is that it is valuable, not just from the point of view of the individual, but from the point of view of the public, that there should be individuals who make such choices.

James thought that every single human being has to make decisions ahead of the evidence of the kind that Pierre had to make, even if they are not as dramatic (of course, this was Sartre's point as well). James argued again and again that our best energies cannot be set free unless we are willing to make the sort of existential commitment that this example illustrates. Someone who acts only when the "estimated utilities" are favorable does not live a meaningful human life. Even if I choose to do something of whose ethical and social value there is absolutely no doubt, say, to devote my life to comforting the dying, or helping the mentally ill, or curing the sick, or relieving poverty, I still have to decide not whether it is good that someone should do that thing, but whether it is good that I, Hilary Putnam, do that thing. The answer to that question cannot be a matter of well-established scientific fact, in however generous a sense of "scientific".

This existentialist note is unmistakable in the quotation from

Fitzjames Stephen with which James ends "The Will to Believe":

> What do you think of yourself? What do you think of the world? These are questions with which all must deal as it seems good to them. They are riddles of the Sphinx, and in some way or other we must deal with them . . . in all important transactions of life we have to take a leap in the dark. If we decide to leave the riddles unanswered, that is a choice. If we waver in our answer, that too is a choice; but whatever choice we make, we make it at our peril. If a man chooses to turn his back altogether on God and the future, no one can prevent him. No one can show beyond reasonable doubt that he is mistaken. If a man thinks otherwise, and acts as he thinks, I do not see how anyone can prove that *he* is mistaken. Each must act as he thinks best, and if he is wrong so much the worse for him. We stand on a mountain pass in the midst of whirling snow and blinding mist, through which we get glimpses now and then of paths which may be deceptive. If we stand still, we shall be frozen to death. If we take the wrong road, we shall be dashed to pieces. We do not certainly know if there is any right one. What must we do? "Be strong and of good courage". Act for the best, hope for the best, and take what comes . . . If death ends all, we cannot meet death better.[19]

James's existentialism is all the more remarkable because he had not read a single existentialist writer (except Nietzsche, whom he pitied,[20] and whom he certainly did not read with any sensitivity). At the same time, James never fails to see the need for a *check* on existential commitment. My right to my own existential commitments stops, for James, where it infringes on the like right of my neighbor. Indeed, the principle of tolerance ("our ancient national doctrine of live and let live") is described by James as having "a far deeper meaning than our people now seem to imagine it to possess".[21] In his Lectures on Religious Belief, Wittgenstein argued that religious belief (insofar as it does not degenerate into superstition) is neither rational nor irrational, and, indeed, the religious people Wittgenstein knew were a pretty gentle lot. But as both Kant and Kierkegaard remind us, there are certain specific diseases of the religious impulse. Kant speaks of fanaticism, idolatry, sorcery, and superstition, and Kierkegaard repeatedly mentions both fanaticism and idolatry, adding that there is the constant danger that the religious person may be worshipping an "idol" even though he or she says all the right words. If reason (or "intelligence") cannot decide what my ultimate commitment should be, it can certainly decide from long and bitter experience that fanaticism is a terrible and destructive thing. In James, a sympathetic understanding of the need for commitment is always tempered by a healthy awareness of the horrors of fanaticism.

If Dewey is not as sensitive to the limits of intelligence as a guide to life as James was, the problem is, perhaps, Dewey's dualistic conception of human goods. For Dewey there are fundamentally two, and only two, dominant dimensions to human life: the social dimension, which for Dewey meant the struggle for a better world, for a better society, and for the release of human potential; and the aesthetic dimension. To the criticism that he saw fundamentally saw all of life as social action, Dewey could and did always reply that, on the contrary, in the last analysis he saw all "consummatory experience" as aesthetic. The trouble with this answer is that a bifurcation of goods into social goods which are attained through the use of instrumental rationality and consummatory experiences which are ultimately aesthetic is too close to the positivist or empiricist division of life into the prediction and control of experiences and the enjoyment of experiences to be adequate. James, I think, succumbs less than Dewey to the temptation to offer a metaphysics of value.

Conclusion

I have in this book been trying to say something about how philosophical reflection can and must go on—about what philosophical reflection can and cannot be. I have argued that the decision of a large part of contemporary analytic philosophy to become a form of metaphysics is a mistake. Indeed, contemporary analytic metaphysics is in many ways a parody of the great metaphysics of the past. As Dewey pointed out, the metaphysics of previous epochs had a vital connection to the culture of those epochs, which is why it was able to change the lives of men and women, and not always for the worse. Contemporary analytic metaphysics has no connection with anything but the "intuitions" of a handful of philosophers. It lacks what Wittgenstein called "weight".

At the same time, I have argued that philosophy must not become a pseudo-scepticism (or nihilism) which announces that it has been discovered that there is no world, no truth, no progress, and so on. My argument has not been directed against technicality—argument and rigorous analysis—nor against engagement with literature. I fully grant that the positivists, for example, did a great service to philosophy by showing how the methods of modern mathematical logic could be used to carry the investigation of a great many philosophical arguments and issues much further than it had been carried before; and the deconstructionists, for all their faults, have called attention to aspects of literature—in particular, to aspects of philosophical literature—which the tradition has neglected. But philosophy cannot be either para-science or para-politics. If I have taken

Wittgenstein as an example of a kind of reflection that avoids both of these temptations, it is because of his relentless honesty and his very real compassion, his constant effort to understand sympathetically forms of life which he himself did not share. If I have taken John Dewey as a model, it is because his reflections on democracy never degenerate into propaganda for the status quo. It is true that the optimism about human potential that Dewey expresses is not something which has been proved to be right, nor does Dewey claim that it has been proved to be right. But, as Dewey emphatically points out, neither has pessimism about human potential been proved to be right. On the contrary, whenever we have given previously oppressed groups a chance to display their capacities, those capacities have surprised us.

I would like to close by saying a little more about this critical dimension of Dewey's thought. When Dewey speaks of using the scientific method to solve social problems he does not mean relying on experts. Dewey emphasizes that, as things are, experts cannot solve social problems. Experts belong to privileged classes and are affected by the rationalizations of which Dewey spoke. They are an elite, and as an elite they are accustomed to telling others what to do to solve their social problems. But the solution to social problems, Dewey argues, requires not that we *tell* other people what to do, but that we release their energies so that they will be able to act for themselves. (An example that comes to mind is the energies that were released when the workers in Poland formed Solidarity.) Dewey's social philosophy is not simply a restatement of classical liberalism; for, as Dewey says, the real fallacy of classical liberalism

> lies in the notion that individuals have such a native or original endowment of rights, powers, and wants that all that

is required on the side of institutions and laws is to eliminate the obstructions they offer to the "free" play of the natural equipment of individuals. The removal of obstructions did have a liberating effect upon such individuals as were antecedently possessed of the means, intellectual and economic, to take advantage of the changed social conditions, but left all others at the mercy of the new social conditions brought about by the free powers of those advantageously situated. The notion that men are equally free to act if only the same legal arrangements apply equally to all—irrespective of differences in education, and command of capital, and that control of the social environment which is furnished by the institution of property—is a pure absurdity, as facts have demonstrated. Since actual, that is effective, rights and demands are products of interactions and are not found in the original and isolated constitution of human nature, whether moral or psychological, mere elimination of obstructions is not enough. The latter merely liberates force and ability as it happens to be distributed by past accidents of history. This "free" action operates disastrously as far as the many are concerned. The only possible conclusion, both intellectually and practically, is that the attainment of freedom conceived as power to act in accord with choice turns upon positive and constructive changes in social arrangements. [22]

We too often forget that Dewey was a radical. But he was a radical *democrat*, not a radical scoffer at "bourgeois democracy". For Dewey the democracy that we have is not something to be spurned, but also not something to be satisfied with. The democracy that we have is an emblem of what could be. What could be is a society which develops the capacities of all its men and women to think for themselves, to participate in the design and testing of social policies, and to judge results. On such a conception, it would be fundamentally misguided to think that majority rule, by itself, amounts to democracy. A majority which does not listen to opinions it finds uncomfortable is not engaging in the intelligent conduct of communal inquiry any more than is an elite which does not allow the majority to decide; and the intelligent conduct of communal inquiry is what democracy is all about, for John Dewey. By the same token, Dewey's civil libertarianism is not a simple giving of priority to something called "freedom" over something called "democracy"; civil liberty is necessary *for* democracy.[23]

I have said something about why I take Wittgenstein as a model, and something about why I take Dewey as a model. Their virtues are in a sense complementary, but I think they have this in common, that Dewey at his best and Wittgenstein at his best illustrate how philosophical reflection which is completely honest can unsettle our prejudices and our pet convictions and our blind spots without flashy claims to "deconstruct" truth itself or the world itself. If the moral of a deconstruction is that *everything* can be "deconstructed", then the deconstruction has no moral. When Wittgenstein, as I read him, deconstructs pet philosophical categories, or when Dewey challenges us to ask how far we are really living our democratic faith, the effect can be to change both our lives and the way we see our lives; and that is the role of philosophical reflection at its best.

NOTES

INDEX

NOTES

1. The Project of Artificial Intelligence

1. Bernard Williams, *Descartes: The Project of Pure Enquiry* (Harmondsworth, Middlesex: Penguin Books, 1978), pp. 245–247. See also Williams' *Ethics and the Limits of Philosophy* (Cambridge, Mass.: Harvard University Press, 1985), where Williams makes sustained use of the notion of an "absolute conception of the world".

2. All this is well described in Justin Webb, *Mechanism, Mentalism and Metamathematics* (Dordrecht: Reidel, 1980).

3. See *The Undecidable: Basic Papers on Undecidable Propositions, Undecidable Problems, and Computable Functions*, ed. Martin Davis (Hewlett, N.Y.: Raven Press, 1965). Turing's was not, however, the first mathematical formulation of the notion of computability; that notion had already been analyzed by Gödel and Herbrand, and Turing showed that his notion was equivalent to theirs.

4. The view I introduced in "The Nature of Mental States" (reprinted in my *Philosophical Papers*, vol. 2, *Mind, Language, and Reality* (Cambridge: Cambridge University Press, 1975) to the effect that the mental states of human beings are to be viewed as simply the computational states of Turing machines, became widely held under the name "functionalism". I explain my reasons for giving it up in detail in *Representation and Reality* (Cambridge, Mass.: MIT Press, 1988).

5. Marian Boykan Pour-El and Ian Richards, "The Wave Equation with Computable Initial Data Such That Its Unique Solution Is Not Computable," *Advances in Mathematics* 39 (1981):215–239.

6. Georg Kreisel, review of paper cited in note 5, *The Journal of Symbolic Logic* 47:4 (1982):900–902.
7. This view is popular with Chomskians, although I am not sure that Noam Chomsky himself would endorse it.
8. I neglect such cases as ceremonial knives, of course.
9. Note that, if one had only appearance to go by, it would be quite natural to regard Great Danes and chihuahuas as animals of different species.
10. This idea was one of the foundation stones of logical positivism. Although the positivists' goal was to reconstruct scientific reasoning rather than to mechanize it, they ran into every one of the problems mentioned here; in many ways the history of Artificial Intelligence is a repeat of the history of logical positivism (the second time as farce?).
11. Nelson Goodman, *Fact, Fiction, and Forecast,* 4th ed. (Cambridge, Mass.: Harvard University Press, 1983).
12. "Much Ado about Not Very Much," *Daedalus* (Winter 1988):269–282.
13. Daniel Dennett, "When Philosophers Encounter Artificial Intelligence," *Daedalus* (Winter 1988):283–295.
14. The best known of these is the "Parallel Distributed Processing" model. See David E. Rummelhart and James L. McLelland and the PDP Research Group, eds., *Parallel Distributed Processing: Explorations in the Microstructure of Cognition,* vols. 1 and 2 (Cambridge, Mass.: MIT Press, 1986).
15. See *The Remembered Present* (Basic Books, 1990).
16. Jerry Fodor, *RePresentations: Philosophical Essays on the Foundations of Cognitive Science* (Cambridge, Mass.: MIT Press, 1981).

2. Does Evolution Explain Representation?

1. See Stephen Jay Gould, *The Panda's Thumb* (New York: Norton, 1980) for a sharp criticism of this sort of Panglossian evolutionism.
2. In my "The Place of Facts in a World of Values," reprinted in *Realism with a Human Face* (Cambridge, Mass: Harvard Uni-

versity Press, 1990), I argue against the view, popular among philosophers, that our ability to discover scientific laws is "explained by evolution". That view is a subtle form of just the mistake criticized in the text.

3. Letter to Herz, 21 Feb. 1772, in *Kant: Philosophical Correspondence, 1759–99*, ed. and trans. Arnulf Zweig, pp. 70–75.

4. Richard Boyd, Jerry Fodor, Ruth Millikan, and Daniel Dennet have suggested the sort of answer which I describe in the text, although each of them has also given other accounts of intentionality which do not depend on evolutionary theory. See Millikan's *Language, Thought and Other Biological Categories* (Cambridge, Mass.: MIT Press, 1984) and Dennett's *Content and Consciousness* (London: Routledge and Kegan Paul, 1969). Fodor's current explanation of intentionality is discussed in Chapter 3.

5. See Fred Dretske, *Knowledge and the Flow of Information* (Cambridge, Mass.: MIT Press, 1981); my criticism of this approach in "Information and the Mental," in E. LePore, ed., *Truth and Interpretation: Perspectives on the Philosophy of Donald Davidson* (Oxford: Basil Blackwell, 1986), pp. 262–271; and Jerry Fodor's criticism in A *Theory of Content and Other Essays* (Cambridge, Mass.: MIT Press, 1990).

6. Daniel Dennett attributes this view to Millikan in "Error, Evolution, and Intentionality," reprinted in *The Intentional Stance* (Cambridge, Mass.: MIT Press, 1987). (I myself do not find it in *Language, Thought, and Other Biological Categories*, although it is compatible with what Millikan writes elsewhere (e.g., the reference to "a wise choice of evolutionary design" in her "Naturalist Reflections on Knowledge," *The Pacific Journal of Philosophy* 65 (1984):314–334.

7. See Ernst Mayr, "Teleological and Teleonomic, a New Analysis," in R. Cohen and M. Wartofsky, eds., *Boston Studies in the Philosophy of Science*, XIV (Dordrecht: Reidel, 1974).

8. When William James claims that the true is what is useful to believe, he doesn't claim that, like dogs, we can't distinguish true from (temporarily) successful beliefs, by the way.

9. Indeed, this point is made by Dennett—who regards intentionality as relative to our "intentional stance"—in the course of praising Ruth Millikan, who thinks precisely the opposite! See "Error, Evolution, and Intentionality."

10. This point seems, in fact, to be well understood by Ruth Millikan. Although in "Naturalist Reflections on Knowledge" she does speak of "evolutionary design" as giving us "mechanisms for forming true beliefs and for learning to form new kinds of true beliefs" (p. 323), in *Language, Thought, and Other Biological Categories*, "evolution" does not even appear as an entry in the index. Instead, her idea is to give an explanation of cultural, not biological, evolution, *in the style of* a Darwinian explanation. The meanings of a word are its different "functions", and each one of these functions becomes stabilized and reproduced because of its ability to serve some goal that is such that (because of various cultural processes) functions that do not serve it tend not to be reproduced, while functions that do serve it tend to be reproduced. The definition of "reproduction" (p. 20) involves counterfactuals ("had A been different with respect to its determinate character p within a specifiable range of variation, as a result, B would have differed accordingly"). Unfortunately, the book makes no real attempt to show that these "functions" can be described in language which does not presuppose the very intentional notions which are supposedly being explained. For example, using "capitulation" *in the sense of* "the act of capitulating" is one of her examples of a function (p. 74). Equally unfortunately, the intentional notions of "specifiability" and of "legitimate explanation" are taken as primitive throughout. Millikan's claim is that the word "cat" refers to cats because a "normal explanation" of how the (undescribed) "function" of that word has been reproduced and stabilized among English speakers would have to refer to a correspondence between that word and cats.

3. A Theory of Reference

1. See Jerry Fodor, *A Theory of Content* (Cambridge, Mass.: MIT Press, 1990). A useful introduction to the theory is Fodor's earlier

"Meaning and the World Order," in *Psychosemantics* (Cambridge, Mass.: MIT Press, 1987), pp. 97–127.

2. To be more precise, Carnap (as of the begining of 1954, which is the last time that we discussed this problem) proposed to define a law as *a logical consequence of fundamental laws,* and a fundamental law as *a true statement of nomological form.* A statement has *nomological form* if it (i) "does not contain space-time coordinate constants, but only variables" (Carnap referred to this as "the Maxwell condition", because it was first formulated by Maxwell); and (ii) satisfies certain further conditions. The exact nature of those further conditions was an unsolved problem, but Carnap thought that fundamental laws would have to be quantitative: "I believe we must find a quantitative language; at least all my attempts of thinking to find a distinction in semantical terms for statements of nomological form fail if we have no quantitative language." With respect to the mathematical form of a fundamental law, Carnap had this to say: "It would be nice if we could say they must have the form of differential equations, but I am not sure we should really require that." (The quotations are from Carnap's notes to a discussion on January 2, 1954, with, in addition to myself, Herbert Feigl, C. G. Hempel, Ernest Nagel, Paul Oppenheim, and Michael Scriven.)

3. See Fodor's essay "Special Sciences," in his *RePresentations: Philosophical Essays on the Foundations of Cognitive Science* (Cambridge, Mass.: MIT Press, 1986), pp. 127–145.

4. If what statement (1) means is that cats cause "cat" tokenings more often than any other one kind of object causes "cat" tokenings, then, of course, we also need a theory of what counts as a "kind" of object—one which does not use any intentional notions.

5. See "Observation Reconsidered," in *A Theory of Content,* esp. p. 237.

6. See David Lewis, *Counterfactuals* (Cambridge, Mass.: Harvard University Press, 1973).

7. In fact, my dog Shlomit frequently eats the apples from our tree; thus, at a certain time of the year the sight of an apple *is* likely to cause "dog" tokening on my part!

8. It has been suggested to me that Fodor might also say that his

theory is meant to apply only to words which have intersubjective stimulus meaning, in Quine's sense. Not only do I not think Fodor would accept this, but the suggestion does not work: if people mistakenly call the same persons superbillionaires because they mistakenly think that certain obvious signs of great wealth indicate superbillionaire status, the word "superbillionaire" will have intersubjective stimulus meaning, but it will not refer to the people to whom it, so to speak, stimulus-refers.

9. Fodor, *Psychosemantics*, p. 66.

10. See Fodor, *The Language of Thought* (Cambridge, Mass.: Harvard University Press, 1989).

11. See the discussion of this word in my *Representation and Reality* (Cambridge, Mass.: MIT Press, 1988).

12. H. L. A. Hart and A. M. Honoré, *Causation in the Law* (Oxford: Clarendon Press, 1959).

13. See my *The Many Faces of Realism*, Lecture I (LaSalle: Open Court, 1987).

14. In *Psychosemantics*, pp. 126–127, Fodor writes that he has "wasted a lot of time that I could have put in sailing" if "the cause" is indeed intentional/semantic.

15. See "Special Sciences," and *Psychosemantics*, esp. pp. 4–6 and pp. 126–127.

16. See *Psychosemantics*, pp. 4–6.

4. Materialism and Relativism

1. See, for example, "Why Is a Philosopher?" in my *Realism with a Human Face* (Cambridge, Mass.: Harvard University Press, 1990).

2. See, for example, Richard Rorty, *Philosophy and the Mirror of Nature* (Princeton: Princeton University Press, 1979), *Consequences of Pragmatism* (Minneapolis: University of Minnesota Press, 1982), and *Contingency, Irony, and Solidarity* (Cambridge: Cambridge University Press, 1989).

3. That is, one whose consequent is entailed by the antecedent together with nomological (physically necessary) statements— statements of exceptionless physical laws.

4. See *Meaning and the Moral Sciences, The Many Faces of Realism*, and "Is the Causal Structure of the Physical Itself Something Physical?"

5. The fact that our relevant interests include knowing certain things—for instance, in the case of the pressure cooker example I used earlier, why the pressure cooker exploded as opposed to functioning "normally", and not why the pressure cooker exploded as opposed to having a hole in its bottom that allows the steam to escape—is what makes the use of causal notions in explaining the notion of reference circular: the notion of knowledge involves the notions of truth and reference. To put it another way, the causal statement is only true or false when a certain framework of pre-understandings is in place, including which conditions should be considered "background conditions" and which conditions should be considered "bringers-about" of effects. But to think of conditions as background conditions or bringers-about of effects one already has to be able to refer. There isn't a distinction in the physical facts themselves between background conditions and bringers-about of effects independent of the existence of human beings with human interests and human capacities.

John Haldane has reminded me that this way of thinking was applied to *all* judgments of fact by Collingwood in his *Autobiography* (Oxford: Oxford University Press, 1939). Collingwood wrote, "What is ordinarily meant when a proposition is called 'true', I thought, was this: *(a)* the proposition belongs to a question-and-answer complex which as a whole is 'true' in the proper sense of the word; *(b)* within this complex it is an answer to a certain question; *(c)* the question is what we ordinarily call a sensible or intelligent question, not a silly one, or in my terminology it 'arises'; *(d)* the proposition is the 'right' answer to the question" (p. 38).

6. Chomsky, *Rules and Representations* (New York: Columbia University Press, (1980), p. 19.

7. Jerry Fodor, *Psychosemantics* (Cambridge, Mass.: MIT Press, 1987), pp. 4–6.

8. See p. xxv of the preface to his *Consequences of Pragmatism*.

9. Rorty said this in a paper he read in Jerusalem, in1987.

10. I consider here and throughout only counterfactuals whose antecedents are supposed to be compatible with physical law. Counterfactuals about what would happen if the laws of physics were different, when they are not simply questions about what would *follow* if the laws of physics were different, are a difficult problem, but not one I need to consider for my present purposes.

11. This purely dialectical function of what look like metaphysical arguments in his prose is stressed by Rorty in *Contingency, Irony, and Solidarity*.

12. Even if they try to escape by controverting the empirical claim that the majority of our cultural peers do not agree that relativism is true, the position is unsatisfactory. While it is not implausible that some philosophical claims can be refuted by some empirical facts, the very fact that *this* philosophical claim can be refuted by the mere fact (if it turns out to be a fact) that the majority of our peers do not agree with it should not make the relativist very happy.

13. Jacques Derrida, *De la grammatologie* (Paris: Editions de Minuit, 1967), p. 18, among other places. In this work, Derrida says *both* that the notion of truth is part of the same belief system as belief in God (who Derrida obviously does not believe exists), and that there is no question of doing without the notion, although we can see that it belongs to an epoch which has reached "closure".

14. Derrida, *Positions*, ed. and annotated by Alan Bass (Chicago: University of Chicago Press, 1981), p. 82.

15. The opposite position is quite consistently taken by Derrida, however—for example, "The sign, by its root and by its implications, is in all its aspects metaphysical" (*Positions*, p. 17); and his reference to "everything that links our language, our culture, our 'system of thought', to the history and system of metaphysics" (*Positions*, p. 20).

16. Ludwig Wittgenstein, *On Certainty* (Oxford: Basil Blackwell, 1969), §519.

17. I do make a stab at doing that in *Reason, Truth, and History* (Cambridge: Cambridge University Press, 1981), however.

18. See my discussion of relativism in *Reason, Truth, and History*.

19. *Philosophical Investigations* (New York: Macmillan, 1953), IIxi, pp. 227ff.
20. I discuss this at greater length in *The Many Faces of Realism*, Lecture 4.
21. Wittgenstein's way of putting this point is that understanding people *(Menschenkenntnis)* is not something everyone can learn. "Can one learn this knowledge? Yes; some can. Not, however, by taking a course in it, but through *'experience'*. —Can someone else be a man's teacher in this? Certainly. From time to time he gives him the right *tip*. —This is what 'learning' and 'teaching' are like here. —What one acquires here is not a technique; one learns correct judgments. There are also rules, but they do not form a system, and only experienced people can apply them right. Unlike calculating rules" (*Philosophical Investigations*, p. 227).
22. I discuss the normativity of the notion of truth at length in *Reason, Truth, and History*.
23. This is summed up in my "Model Theory and the 'Factuality' of Semantics," in *Reflections on Chomsky*, ed. Alex George (Oxford: Oxford University Press, 1989).
24. See *Reason, Truth, and History*, chap. 2 and Appendix.

5. Bernard Williams and the Absolute Conception of the World

1. *Ethics and the Limits of Philosophy* (Cambridge, Mass.: Harvard University Press, 1985): *Descartes: The Project of Pure Enquiry* (Harmondsworth, Middlesex: Penguin Books, 1978). See also Williams' *Moral Luck* (Cambridge: Cambridge University Press, 1981), esp. chap. 11, "The Truth in Relativism".
2. "Cognitivism" in ethical theory is the view that ethical judgments can be true and false.
3. Williams rejects the Kuhnian notion of incommensurability in science, but he finds it useful in ethics. See *Ethics*, pp. 157–158.
4. Ibid., chaps. 8 and 9.
5. *Descartes*, pp. 236–249. See also pp. 298–303.
6. Of course, one is also allowed to use terms defined with the aid

of the primary qualities, as, for example, "momentum" is defined with the aid of "mass" and "velocity", and "velocity" is defined in terms of "time" and "position".

7. *Descartes*, pp. 243–246.

8. Descartes claimed that interaction between the body and the soul, which he placed in the pineal gland, would preserve the conservation of total momentum, but he was unaware that the laws of physics require also that momentum *in each direction* be conserved, and this must be violated if the interaction is to divert the body from the trajectory it would have followed anyway.

9. Under the influence of Quine and Davidson, Williams expresses scepticism as to whether intentional content can be part of the absolute description. "If the various sorts of considerations which have been summarily sketched here are correct, then we have to give up not just dualism but the belief in the determinacy of the mental. These considerations converge on the conclusion that there are no fully determinate contents of the world which are its psychological contents" (*Descartes*, p. 300).

10. Ibid., p. 247.

11. See "The Fixation of Belief," in Charles Hartshorne and Paul Weiss, eds., *Collected Papers of Charles Sanders Peirce*, vol. 5, *Pragmatism and Pragmaticism*, pp. 223–247 (Cambridge, Mass.: Harvard University Press, 1965).

12. *Descartes*, pp. 302–303.

13. The absolute conception "will also help to explain to us, *though not necessarily to those alien investigators*, such things as our capacity to grasp that conception" (*Ethics*, p. 140; emphasis added).

14. I discuss this at more length in "Objectivity and the Science/Ethics Distinction," reprinted in *Realism with a Human Face* (Cambridge, Mass.: Harvard University Press, 1990). I have adapted a few paragraphs from that earlier essay here.

15. The Spanish philosopher Ortega y Gassett had pointed this out in 1923. See "Introducción a la estimativa," in his *Obras Completas* (Madrid: Revista de Occidente, 1958), vol. 6, pp. 317 and 320–321.

16. John McDowell, "Are Moral Requirements Hypothetical Imperatives," *Proceedings of the Aristotelian Society*, suppl. vol. 52 (1978) and "Virtue and Reason," *Monist* 62 (1979).
17. *Ethics*, pp. 145–146.
18. Ibid., p. 142.
19. I would agree with Williams that utterances in a hypertraditional society cannot be analyzed as conjunctions of value-neutral descriptive claims and claims involving the thin ethical concepts *right* and *wrong*, but I have criticized the claim that such utterances do not even *imply* any claims involving our thin ethical concepts in "Can Ethics Be Ahistorical? The French Revolution and the Holocaust," in *Culture and Modernity: The Authority of the Past*, Proceedings of the Sixth East-West Philosophers' Conference, edited by Len Goodman.
20. Witty saying credit: Alan Garfinkle.
21. *Moral Luck*, p. 141.
22. In some contexts, the counterpart of ordinary-language "heat" is quantity of heat rather than temperature; but the seventeenth-century discussion usually turns around comparisons of temperature.
23. See his *Color for Philosophers* (Indianapolis, Ind.: Hackett, 1986).
24. "XIV. Neurology," in *Quarterly Progress Report no. 87* (Research Laboratory of Electronics, M.I.T.: 1967). A similar view is presented by David Hilbert in *Color and Color Perception: A Study in Anthropocentric Realism* (Stanford: Center for the Study of Language and Information, 1990).
25. *Color: Some Philosophical Problems from Wittgenstein*. (Oxford: Blackwell, 1991).
26. For example, in *Fact, Fiction, and Forecast* (Cambridge, Mass.: Harvard University Press, 1983), Goodman shows that "grue" (green and examined prior to *t* or blue and not examined prior to *t*) is disjunctive if we take "green" and "blue" as primitive, but "green" is disjunctive in exactly the same way if we take "grue" and "bleen" as primitive.
27. Charles W. Misner, Kip S. Thorne, and John Archibald Wheeler, *Gravitation* (San Fransisco: W. H. Freeman, 1973), pp. 23–29.

28. See his *Experience and Nature* (LaSalle, Ind.: Open Court, 1926).

29. One camp—the "left-wing Sellarsians"—would abandon the notion of "picturing" altogether. Richard Rorty belongs to this camp. Right-wing Sellarsians would retain the notion.

30. *Ethics*, p. 140

31. *Descartes*, p. 299.

32. This is so even granting that the truth conditions of a sentence are not completely fixed by the conditions for its warranted assertability; for if translation is determinate at least up to conditions of warranted assertability, then ascriptions of content are very strongly constrained. My own view, argued in *Reason, Truth, and History* and in the last chapter of *Representation and Reality* is that truth conditions are fixed by conditions of warranted assertability together with conditions of the form "epistemic conditions A are better than epistemic conditions B for making judgments of warranted assertability about S". Note that these latter conditions are also normative. Of course, a metaphysical realist might hold that (what we take to be) conditions of warranted assertability do not constrain truth conditions *at all*; but I do not believe that this can be a position Williams would find congenial.

33. See, for example, *Contingency, Irony, and Solidarity* (Cambridge: Cambridge University Press, 1989), pp. 3–22, and "Pragmatism, Davidson and Truth" in E. Lepore, ed., *Truth and Interpretation: Perspectives on the Philosophy of Donald Davidson* (Oxford: Blackwell, 1986), esp. pp. 341–342.

34. See *Ethics*, p. 148, and the discussion leading up to it.

35. Ibid., p. 143.

36. In particular, Williams cannot mean that it "lapses" in only a pragmatic sense, since the contrast he draws with the scientific case would then make no sense. "When relativism is rejected in a given area, this does not mean that there are no notional confrontations. The confrontation between phlogiston theory and any contemporary theory of combustion is without doubt notional, and phlogiston theory is not now a real option; but on the nonrelativist view of such theories there is something to be said

in appraisal of phlogiston theory, that it is false" (*Ethics*, pp. 161–162). This immediately follows his explanation of what he means by "taking a relativist view" toward ethical conflicts: that it is only in the case of real conflicts that the language of appraisal can be used. Since "false" (and, by implication, "true") is "something to be said in appraisal", Williams clearly continues to hold the view that the question of truth lapses in ethics (but not in science) when the conflict is notional.

37. One of the anonymous referees of this book for the Harvard University Press suggested that this is how Williams could respond to the "blatant contradiction".

38. This is prohibited by the Talmud.

39. *Ethics*, p. 148.

40. Williams is quite deliberate about this. "In introducing this kind of relativism, I have mentioned ethical outlooks rather than particular practices, and it is to fairly large-scale systems or bodies of beliefs and attitudes that it has to be applied" (*Ethics*, p. 162).

6. Irrealism and Deconstruction

1. See Richard Rorty, *Consequences of Pragmatism* (Minneapolis: University of Minnesota Press, 1982), pp. 90–109.

2. This has been urged by Saul Kripke, in *Naming and Necessity* (Cambridge, Mass.: Harvard University Press, 1980).

3. I should emphasize that, for Goodman, versions do not have to be formalized, although the differences between versions tend to come out more sharply if we do formalize them to some extent.

4. "So many rival formulations are proposed in all the branches of science that investigators have become accustomed to the notion that no theory is absolutely a transcript of reality . . . They are only a man-made language, a conceptual shorthand, as someone calls them, in which we write our reports of nature; and languages, as is well known, tolerate much choice of expression and many dialects." *Pragmatism and the Meaning of Truth* (Cam-

bridge, Mass.: Harvard University Press, 1978), with introduction by A. J. Ayer, p. 33.

5. See "Works, Words, Worlds," The first chapter in Nelcon Goodman, *Ways of Worldmaking* (Indianapolis: Hackett, 1979).

6. Goodman's reply to talks by myself and Scheffler is reprinted, titled "Starmaking," in his *On Mind and Other Matters* (Cambridge, Mass.: Harvard University Press, 1984), pp. 39–44. Unfortunately, the printed version leaves out the Big Dipper example. My talk, "Reflections on Goodman's *Ways of Worldmaking*," is reprinted in my *Realism with a Human Face* (Cambridge, Mass.: Harvard University Press, 1990); Scheffler's talk appears in *Synthese* 45 (1980):201–209, with a reply by Goodman, pp. 211–215.

7. This form of the objection is from Avishai Margalit (in conversation).

8. Water, for example, is not really just H_2O: real water always contains H_4O_2, H_6O_3 . . . as well as D_2O, D_4O_2, D_6O_3 . . . as well as superpositions (in the quantum mechanical sense) of all of the foregoing. Suppose one had a bowl full of H_4O_2; would it be a bowl of *water?*

9. Indeed, elementary particles may not even be *relativistically invariant*. On this, see P. C. W. Davies, "Elementary Particles Do Not Exist," in *Quantum Theory of Gravitation*, ed. Steven M. Christensen (London: Adam Helger Ltd., 1984).

10. Note to fans of possible-worlds semantics: when I say that our linguistic practices made him Joe Ullian, I am using "Joe Ullian" non-rigidly (it is to indicate this that I put quotation marks around "Joe Ullian" in the text). The "rigid" use is not relevant here; speaking in terms of rigid designation, one cannot even say that our linguistic practices made the Big Dipper the Big Dipper.

11. See "Lecture One: Is There Still Anything to Say About Reality and Truth," in *The Many Faces of Realism* (LaSalle, Ind.: Open Court, 1985); "A Defense of Internal Realism" and "Truth and Convention," in *Realism with a Human Face*.

12. I say "concrete" because those who take this view sometimes refer to space-time as the "matter" of which everything is made, and

think of the space-time points as the ultimate "atoms" of which this matter consists.

13. That points in space are "mere limits" was the view of Kant in the *Critique of Pure Reason* (see the Second Antinomy).

14. The idea that points in space are mere limits can be formalized by identifying points with *equivalence classes of convergent series of spheres*. A series of spheres is convergent if (1) each sphere (except the first) is contained in the preceding sphere; and (2) the radius of the i-th sphere approaches 0 as *i* increases without limit. Two series are *equivalent* if any sphere in either series contains all the spheres after the i-th, for some *i*, in the other. This way of formalizing Kant's intuitive idea is due to Whitehead, in Whitehead and Russell's *Principia Mathematica*.

15. Davidson, "The Very Idea of a Conceptual Scheme," in his *Inquiries into Truth and Interpretation* (Oxford: Oxford University Press, 1985). This does not mention Goodman by name, but Quine's review of Goodman's *Fact, Fiction and Forecast*, in *Theories and Things*, (Cambridge, Mass.: Harvard University Press, 1981) takes a similar line. See also Quine's reference to Davidson in his rejection of conceptual relativism (which he refers to as "the ecumenical point of view") in "Reply to Roger F. Gibson, Jr.," in *The Philosophy of W. V. Quine*, ed. L. Hahn and P.A. Schilpp (LaSalle, Ind.: Open Court, 1986), pp. 155–157.

16. See Quine, "Things and Their Place in Theories," in *Theories and Things*, esp. pp. 21–22.

17. For an analysis of the notion of equivalence involved, see "Equivalence" in my *Philosophical Papers*, vol. 3; *Realism and Reason* (Cambridge: Cambridge University Press, 1983).

18. See Goodman, *The Structure of Appearance* (Dordrecht: Reidel, 1977), first published in 1951.

19. The fact that we cannot say that a sentence in the one version has the same "meaning" as either (1) its "translation" into the other version, or (2) the sentence with the very same spelling in the other version, does not mean we are stuck with just saying that the two versions are *incommensurable*. Rather it is that we

treat a sentence and its "translation" as if they had the same meaning, even though ordinary translation practice does not sanction doing so.

20. Taking points to be sets of *concentric* spheres is still another way of formalizing the idea that points are "mere limits". If one adopts this way, then "identity" of points has to be reinterpreted as *equivalence* in the sense proposed in note 14.

21. Speaking in this way about "correct descriptions of a situation" does not commit me to thinking of situations as having precise boundaries ("he stood roughly there" can be a perfectly good description of a situation), or to treating situations as the ultimate metaphysical realities. Situation-language is just one *more* way of talking that it is sometimes convenient to employ.

22. Derrida goes on to say "the word 'signifier' leads us back to or retains us in the logocentric circle . . . I have already told you what I think about the notion of the signifier. The same holds for the notions of *representation* and *subject*". *Positions*, ed. and annotated by Alan Bass (Chicago: University of Chicago Press, 1981), pp. 82–83.

23. See my "A Defense of Internal Realism," in *Realism with a Human Face*.

24. A *Course in General Linguistics* (first published in 1916), translated and annotated by Roy Harris (LaSalle, Ind.: Open Court, 1986), with the original pagination indicated in the margins.

25. In *Positions*, pp. 15–36.

26. Derrida is here quoting from Saussure's *Cours de linguistique generale*, p. 145.

27. Derrida is quoting from ibid., p. 164.

28. Note that in French semiology the "signified" is the sense, or intension of the signifier, not its extension. Derrida is saying that in translation we speak as if there were a "meaning" that two different signs could share.

29. I don't, of course, mean to suggest any causal influence here. Derrida's position was worked out long before Goodman turned "irrealist".

30. *Ways of Worldmaking*, pp. 139–140.

31. One reason this is a misinterpretation is that Derrida himself stresses that the logocentric predicament is not a "pathology" for which he is offering us a cure; it is rather, a predicament we are fated to be in. See *De la grammatologie* (Paris: Editions de Minuit, 1967). At the same time, however, notions that "retain us in" the logocentric predicament are spoken of as having "collapsed", as we saw above.

32. Derrida, "The Principle of Reason: The University in the Eyes of Its Pupils," *Diacritics* 13 (1983):44.

33. *The Ear of the Other*, trans. Christie V. McDonald (New York: Schocken Books, 1985), pp. 23–24.

34. "Serious Play: The Ethical-Political Horizon of Jacques Derrida," *The Journal of Speculative Philosophy* 1:2 (1987):93–117. The quotation is from p. 111.

7. Wittgenstein on Religious Belief

1. David Lewis, *Counterfactuals* (Cambridge, Mass.: Harvard University Press, 1973), p. 88.

2. Lewis thinks it is fixed primarily by an "eliteness" or "naturalness" metric over kinds which belongs to the nature of reality itself, independent of our interests. For references and a discussion see the next-to-last chapter of my *Representation and Reality* (Cambridge, Mass.: MIT Press, 1988).

3. The suggestion advanced by Paul and Patricia Churchland that we reject "folk psychology" as, in effect, mythology, and the suggestion advanced by Paul Churchland that we need "a successor concept to the notion of truth" are good examples of this. For references and a discussion see chap. 4 of *Representation and Reality*.

4. Ludwig Wittgenstein, *Lectures and Conversations on Aesthetics, Psychology and Religious Belief*, ed. Cyril Barrett (Berkeley: University of California Press, 1966).

5. Ibid., p. 53.

6. Ibid.

7. Ibid.

8. Ibid., p. 54.
9. Wittgenstein also said in the first lecture, "It has been said a thousand times, and by intelligent people, that indubitability is not enough in this case [Christianity]. Even if there is as much evidence as for Napoleon. Because the indubitability wouldn't be enough to make me change my whole life. It doesn't rest on a historic basis (in the sense that the ordinary belief in historic facts could serve as a foundation)" (p. 57). Compare this with what Søren Kierkegaard said about the historical argument in the *Concluding Unscientific Postscript* (Princeton, N.J.: Princeton University Press, 1941), pp. 25–48. When Wittgenstein writes "intelligent people" is he speaking of Kierkegaard?
10. Kierkegaard, *Concluding Unscientific Postscript*, p. 53.
11. Wittgenstein, *Lectures*, pp. 54–55.
12. Ibid., p. 55.
13. Ibid., p. 56.
14. Ibid., p. 55.
15. Ibid., p. 63.
16. Ibid.
17. Ibid., p. 59.
18. Ibid., pp. 60–61.
19. Ibid., p. 53.
20. Ibid.
21. Ibid., p. 58.
22. Ibid. I have rectified the quotation marks.
23. Ibid., p. 70.
24. Stanley Cavell, *The Claim of Reason* (Oxford: Oxford University Press, 1979), pp. 247–291.
25. See Stanley Cavell "Existentialism and Analytic Philosophy," in *Themes out of School* (San Francisco: North Point Press, 1984).
26. I want to acknowledge that I have been very much aided in arriving at this understanding of Kierkegaard by the Cavell essay cited in the previous note, and also by a study by James Conant, "Kierkegaard, Wittgenstein and Nonsense," in *Pursuits of Reason: Essays Presented to Stanley Cavell*, ed. T. Cohen, P. Guyer, and H. Putnam (Lubbock, Tex.: Texas Tech University Press, 1992),

in which he compares the exegetical difficulties in reading Wittgenstein's *Tractatus* and those we face in reading Kierkegaard's *Concluding Unscientific Postscript*. I do not, of course, assume that either Cavell or Conant would necessarily agree with the formulations here.

27. Wittgenstein, *Lectures*, pp. 71–72.

28. Wittgenstein, *Culture and Value* (Chicago: University of Chicago Press, 1980), p. 83.

29. See, for example, lecture 25 in Wittgenstein's *Lectures on the Philosophy of Mathematics*, ed. Cora Diamond (Chicago: University of Chicago Press, 1989).

30. James Conant has suggested to me that one should also consider the metaphor of "gripping" involved in "being in the grip of a picture". The suggestion is that philosophical pictures *constrain* rather than liberate, perhaps.

8. Wittgenstein on Reference and Relativism

1. Wittgenstein, *Lectures and Conversations on Aesthetics, Psychology, and Religious Belief* (Berkeley: University of California Press, 1966), p. 66.

2. Again we notice that Wittgenstein has no hostility at all to pictures as such, or to the idea of connecting words with pictures.

3. Wittgenstein, *Lectures*, p. 67.

4. I should note here in passing that Kripke and I have both denied quite consistently that what we are proposing is a theory of reference in Fodor's sense, that is to say, a definition of reference in causal terms. What Kripke and I have defended is the idea that certain sorts of words can refer only if there is a causal connection between them and certain things or certain kinds of things. But we have never tried to *reduce* reference to causation.

5. In relativity theory, my light cone consists of all the events from which a signal (traveling at subluminal velocity or at the speed of light) could have been sent to me now (my "absolute past") together with all the events which a signal sent out by me now (at subluminal velocity or at the speed of light) could reach in

the future (my "absolute future"). Events outside my light cone are such that they can be neither causes nor effects of what is happening now, since no causal signal can travel faster than light.

6. See Richard Boyd, "Materialism without Reductionism: What Physicalism Does Not Entail," in Ned Block, ed., *Readings in Philosophy of Psychology*, vol. 1 (Cambridge, Mass.: Harvard University Press, 1980).

7. Hartry Field, "Tarski's Theory of Truth," *The Journal of Philosophy*, 69:13 (1972):347–375.

8. Wittgenstein, *Lectures*, p. 68.

9. See Rush Rhees's review of George Pitcher, *The Philosophy of Wittgenstein*, in Rhees, *Discussions of Wittgenstein* (London: Routledge and Kegan Paul, 1970).

10. "Bemerkungen zu Frazers *Golden Bough*," ed. Rush Rhees, *Synthese* 17 (1967):233–253.

11. Wittgenstein, *On Certainty* (Oxford: Basil Blackwell, 1969), §605: "But what if the physicist's statement were superstition, and it were just as absurd to go by it in reaching a verdict as to go by an ordeal by fire?"

12. Throughout this chapter, references by section number are to *On Certainty*.

13. See "The Question of Linguistic Idealism," in *From Parmenides to Wittgenstein: The Collected Philosophical Papers of G. E. M. Anscombe*, vol. 1 (Minneapolis: University of Minnesota Press, 1981).

14. See the discussion of relativism in chap. 5 of *Reason, Truth, and History*.

15. See my "Introducing Cavell," in *Pursuits of Reason: Essays Presented to Stanley Cavell*, Ted Cohen, Paul Guyer, and Hilary Putnam, eds. (Lubbock: Texas Tech University Press, 1992).

9. A Reconsideration of Deweyan Democracy

1. Bernard Williams, *Ethics and the Limits of Philosophy*, (Cambridge, Mass.: Harvard University Press, 1985), pp. 26–27.

2. Although Williams also considers the Kantian strategy, he concludes that it is unworkable, and that if any objective justification could be given—which he doubts—it would have to be along Aristotelian lines. See chap. 3 in Williams, *Ethics*.
3. Ibid., p. 45.
4. Ibid., pp. 45–46.
5. "Towards the Decolonization of the Mind," in Frédérique Apffel Marglin and Stephen A. Marglin, eds., *Dominating Knowledge* (Oxford: Oxford University Press, 1991).
6. John Dewey and James H. Tufts, *Ethics*, rev. ed. (New York: Henry Holt, 1932), p. 385.
7. These arguments are set forth in Alasdair MacIntyre, *After Virtue* (Notre Dame, Ind.: Notre Dame University Press, 1980) and its successor, *Whose Justice? Which Rationality?* (Notre Dame, Ind.: Notre Dame University Press, 1988).
8. In this respect Dewey differs radically from Habermas, who in many ways agrees with Dewey that democracy is a prerequisite for rational social decision making with respect to ends as well as with respect to means, but wishes to establish this by a "transcendental argument". For a discussion of the similarities and differences between Dewey's views and those of Habermas and K.O. Apel, see the version of this chapter published in the *Southern California Law Review* 63 (1990):1681–1688.
9. "How to Make Our Ideas Clear" and "The Fixation of Belief," reprinted in *Collected Papers of Charles Sanders Peirce*, vol. 5, *Pragmatism and Pragmaticism*, ed. Charles Hartshorne and Paul Weiss (Cambridge, Mass.: Harvard University Press, 1965).
10. For an elaboration of this claim see Hilary Putnam and Ruth Anna Putnam, "Dewey's *Logic:* Epistemology as Hypothesis," in *Transactions of the C. S. Peirce Society* 26:4 (1990):407–434.
11. John Dewey, *Experience and Nature* (LaSalle, Ind.: Open Court, 1926), pp. 407–408.
12. Emile Durkheim, "Individualism and the Intellectuals" (1898), reprinted with an introduction by Steven Lukes in *Political Studies* 17 (1969):14–30.

13. *The Moral Writings of John Dewey*, ed. James Gouinlock (New York: Hafner/Macmillan, 1976) p. 245 (originally from *The Public and its Problems*, 206–209).
14. Jean-Paul Sartre, *Existentialisme est un humanisme*, trans. Philip Mairet (London: Methuen, 1968).
15. A similar point is made by Ruth Anna Putnam in "Weaving Seamless Webs," *Philosophy* 62 (1987):207–220. The example she uses is that of a pacifist who has to decide whether and to what extent he is willing to participate in the war effort, for example by serving in a non-combatant capacity. As she says, "sometimes only within the frame of a whole life, and sometimes only within the frame of the life of a whole community, can these decisions be evaluated" (p. 216).
16. James makes this explicit in chap. 8 of *The Meaning of Truth* (1909), particularly in footnote 9, where he writes "whether the pragmatic theory of truth is true *really*, they [the pragmatists] cannot warrant—they can only believe it. To their hearers they can only propose it, as I propose it to my readers, as something to be verified *ambulando*, or by the way in which its consequences may confirm it". *Pragmatism and the Meaning of Truth* (Cambridge, Mass.: Harvard University Press, 1975), p. 281.
17. E. A. Singer, Jr., describes the reaction of the graduate students in *Modern Thinkers and Present Problems* (New York: Henry Holt, 1923), pp. 218–220.
18. This is not to say that religious belief is unwarranted. What I myself believe is that it is "warranted", though not by evidence. This stance is intimately connected with the sense of existential decision.
19. James, "The Will to Believe," in *The Will to Believe*, first published in 1897 (Cambridge, Mass.: Harvard University Press, 1975), p. 33. James is quoting from Fitzjames Stephen, *Liberty, Equality, Fraternity* (London: Smith, Elder, 1874).
20. See James, *Varieties of Religious Experience*, first published in 1902 (Cambridge, Mass.: Harvard University Press, 1985), pp. 296–297, on "poor Nietzsche".
21. James, *Talks to Teachers on Psychology*, first published in 1899

(Cambridge, Mass.: Harvard University Press, 1983), p. 5. The entire concluding paragraph of the preface, from which this quotation is taken, is a paean to tolerance and an attack on "the pretension of our nation to inflict its own inner ideals and institutions *vi et armis* upon Orientals" (James was referring to the Philippines).

22. Dewey, "Philosophies of Freedom," in H. M. Kallen, ed., *Freedom in the Modern World* (New York: Coward-McCann, 1928), pp. 236–271; quoted passage on pp. 249–250.

23. Thus constitutional restictions on the unlimited exercise of majority power, such as the Bill of Rights, are not a limitation of "democracy" in Dewey's sense, but a protection of it.

Index

Absolute conception of the world: and physics, 2, 35, 80–84, 90, 92, 93, 95–98, 105–106, 107; and ethical judgments, 80–81, 87–91, 106, 153; and special science, 83–85, 91–98, 102, 105–106; and explanation of perspectives, 84–85, 98–101; and convergence of perspectives, 84–85, 101–103. *See also* Perspectives

Artificial Intelligence: and computationalism, 3–7, 16–19; and induction, 8–14; and background knowledge, 9–10, 12–14; and similarity problem, 10–11; and language learning, 14–16. *See also* Computationalism; Cognitive science

Amish, 106–107

Anscombe, Elizabeth, 173

Anthropology, 183

Aristotle, 72, 181–182

Asymmetric dependence. *See* Causation; Counterfactuals

Austin, J. L., 98

Aztecs, 106

Barrett, Cyril, 158

Behaviorism, 15

Berlin, Isaiah, 140

Bernstein, Richard, 131–132

Biology, 35, 83, 90; and counterfactuals, 50–51, 55, 58, 66. *See also* Evolution

Bloom, Allan: *The Closing of the American Mind*, 185

Boyd, Richard, 162

Carnap, Rudolf: on inductive logic, 11–12, 129; on scientific laws, 35

Causation: and reference, 3, 23–24, 35–55, 108, 140–141, 159–167, 168; and counterfactuals, 33–34, 35–47, 50–52, 61–66; in physics, 34, 50–55, 57, 70; and asymmetric dependence, 38–47; ordinary language, 47–48, 50, 58–59, 78; contributory, 48–49, 50, 65; intentionality of, 50, 57–58; interest relativity of, 61–66; and truth, 77–78. *See also* Counterfactuals

Cavell, Stanley, 75, 178; *The Claim of Reason*, 153, 177–178

Chomsky, Noam: on language learning, 14–15; on language use, 16–17; on causation, 64–65

Cognitive science: and Artificial Intelligence, 3–18, 21; and computationalism, 3–7, 16–19, 22; and evolutionary theory, 3, 19–34; and causal theories of reference, 3, 34, 35–59. *See also*

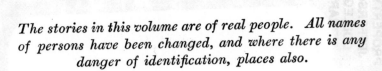

The stories in this volume are of real people. All names of persons have been changed, and where there is any danger of identification, places also.